Jessie P. Van Zile Belden

Concerning Some of the Ancestors and Descendants

of Royal Denison Belden and Olive Cadwell Belden

Jessie P. Van Zile Belden

Concerning Some of the Ancestors and Descendants
of Royal Denison Belden and Olive Cadwell Belden

ISBN/EAN: 9783337161415

Printed in Europe, USA, Canada, Australia, Japan

Cover: Foto ©Andreas Hilbeck / pixelio.de

More available books at **www.hansebooks.com**

CONCERNING SOME OF THE ANCESTORS AND DESCENDANTS OF

Royal Denison Belden

and

Olive Cadwell Belden

BY

JESSIE PERRY VAN ZILE BELDEN

Printed for Private Circulation

BY J. B. LIPPINCOTT COMPANY, PHILADELPHIA

MDCCCXCVIII

Bayldon

IN LOVING MEMORY

OF

Augustus Cadwell Belden,

WHO BORE HIS PART IN LIFE'S STRUGGLE WITH COURAGE,

WITH UNSWERVING HONESTY AND UNSULLIED

HONOR, AND OF WHOM IT

WAS SAID,

" HE WAS ALWAYS TRUE AND LOYAL, AND HIS

DEATH IS A PUBLIC LOSS."

JAMES JEROME BELDEN.
JESSIE VAN ZILE BELDEN.

"Out of monuments, names, words, proverbs, traditions, private records and evidences, fragments of stories, passages of books that concern not story and the like, we save and recover somewhat from the deluge of time."

Authorities

❧❧❧

History of England, Macaulay.
History of the United States, Bryant.
History of the United States, Prescott.
History of Deerfield, Sheldon.
Memorial History of Hartford County, Trumbull.
History of Hadley, Judd.
History of New London.
History of Northfield, Temple and Sheldon.
History and Proceedings of the Pocumtuck Valley Memorial
Association, Vol. I.
Genealogical History of New England, Savage.
New England Register.
Puritan Settlers of Connecticut, Hinman.
Register of the First Settlers of New England, Farmer.
Onondaga's Centennial, D. H. Bruce.
Published Revolutionary War Records of Massachusetts, Vol. I.
Foote Genealogy.
Hall Ancestry.
Lyman Genealogy.
Stanton Genealogy.
Wilkinson Genealogy.
Archives at Bureau of Pensions, Washington, D. C.
Archives at University of the State of New York.
Colonial Records of the State of Connecticut.
Colonial War Records of Massachusetts.
Massachusetts Archives.
Records of the Colony of Massachusetts Bay.

Authorities

Town, Probate, and Church Records of

Branford, Connecticut.
East Hartford, Connecticut.
Guilford, Vermont.
Hartford, Connecticut.
Hatfield, Massachusetts.
Northfield, Massachusetts.
Wethersfield, Connecticut.
Whately, Massachusetts.
Winchester, New Hampshire.

Special Thanks for Information are Due

Hon. Morris K. Beardsley, Bridgeport, Connecticut.
Miss Agnes W. Belden, Newington, Connecticut.
Miss Esther E. Bidwell, Wethersfield, Connecticut.
Doctor F. A. Castle, New York City.
Mrs. Ephraim Chamberlain, Utica, New York.
F. W. Chamberlain, Esq., Montclair, New Jersey.
Doctor C. D. Davis, Winchester, New Hampshire.
Captain Edward Hooker, United States Navy.
Mrs. A. A. Ketchum, Dover Plains, New York.
Hon. Wm. M. Olin, Boston, Massachusetts.
Rev. C. B. Selleck, Norwalk, Connecticut.
Hon. George W. Sheldon, Deerfield, Massachusetts.
Captain Luis F. Emilio, New York City.

Many other persons have been consulted for reminiscences, and careful examination has been given private records, family Bibles, inscriptions on gravestones, and deeds and wills.

Various Forms of the Name used in this Branch of the Belden Family

Bayldon
Until 1641

Belden
1641 to 1643

Belding
1643 to 1736

Belden
1736 to 1753

Belding
1753 to 1825

Belden
1825 to present time

List of Illustrations

✤✤✤

List of Illustrations

List of Illustrations

List of Illustrations

FOREWORD

✸✸

THE history of the Bayldon family, including the American descendants called Belden and Belding, covers a period of more than eight hundred years,— from before the battle of Hastings, in 1066, to the present time.

The following record of one branch of the family has been compiled from many sources.

The genealogical part will enable other branches to follow out their own lines by correspondence with town-clerks and search of probate records.

The English data requires something more than a mere mention of its source. It would have been impossible to have obtained certain records and illustrations without the assistance of our consul at Leeds, Mr. Norfleet Harris, Mr. Morkill, of Austhorpe Lodge, Mr. Alexander Hasse, of Leeds and Baildon, and Mr. William Paley Baildon, F.S.A.

Mr. Baildon is a barrister, member of the council of the Yorkshire Archæological Society, and Fellow of the Society of Antiquaries. His collection of Baildon data, when published under the title of "Baildon and the Baildons" (taking the family back to Runic tombstones), will be the most complete history of a family in existence. He has spent his summers for twenty years in searching registers, wills, etc., in Yorkshire, and has twenty manuscript volumes and many sketch-books containing Baildon data. These records were placed at my disposal, and permission given me to copy whatever would be of service.

Mr. Baildon is the grandson of Archbishop Paley, and his house is filled with Paley and Baildon heirlooms. The English illustrations, with the exception of those of Baildon and Kippax, were his choice and made under his supervision, and I am particularly indebted to him for the reproduction of the old deed of the twelfth century, the copy of the stained-glass window in Methley Hall, the photographs from the British Museum, the portraits of William and Francis Baildon, and the pedigrees.

The Bayldon coat of arms, represented on the cover, is a reproduction of the one in the British Museum, and was registered at the Herald's visitation of Yorkshire in 1585.

The following reference can be found in " Foster's Visitation of Yorkshire" :

SKYRACK.

BAYLDON OF BAYLDON.

Arms :—Argent ; a fesse between three fleur-de-lis sable.

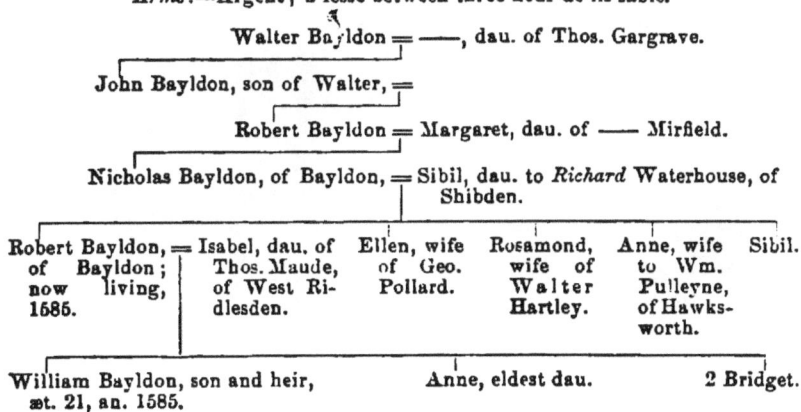

Walter Bayldon = ——, dau. of Thos. Gargrave.

John Bayldon, son of Walter, =

Robert Bayldon = Margaret, dau. of —— Mirfield.

Nicholas Bayldon, of Bayldon, = Sibil, dau. to *Richard* Waterhouse, of Shibden.

Robert Bayldon, of Bayldon; now living, 1585. = Isabel, dau. of Thos. Maude, of West Ridlesden.	Ellen, wife of Geo. Pollard.	Rosamond, wife of Walter Hartley.	Anne, wife to Wm. Pulleyne, of Hawksworth.	Sibil.

William Bayldon, son and heir, æt. 21, an. 1585.

Anne, eldest dau.

2 Bridget.

(Signed) ROBERT BAILDON.

ffforeworð

BAYLDON OF BAYLDON

Argent; a fesse between three fleur-de-lis *sable*.
Another:
Argent; a fesse between three fleur-de-lis *gules*.
Another—Cecilie, daughter of Bayldon of Bayldon:
Argent; a chevron between three fleur-de-lis sable; from the chief a pile descending to the top of the chevron. Cecilie married James Rawson, of Fryston.

The coat of arms in the possession of the descendants of Richard Bayldon, of Wethersfield, has the addition of the motto, "God my leader."

J. P. V. Z. Belden.

Part 1

❧

Historical

BAYLDON COAT OF ARMS

From the original in the British Museum

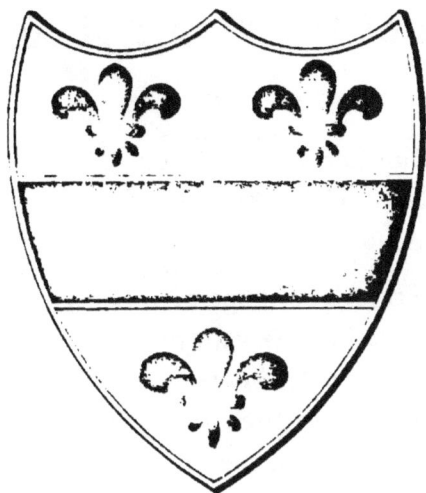

Origin of the Name of Baildon

❦❦❦

THE following is a portion of a letter written by J. M. N. Colls, Esq., to Edward Hailstone, Esq., F.S.A., of Bradford:

"MY DEAR SIR,—The range of hills lying north by west of Bradford separating the valleys of the rivers Wharfe and Aire form an extremely interesting field of research. . . . The range of mountains from Ilkley and Otley on the north to Baildon and Bingley on the south evidently formed a large tract for a length of seven miles and south, which subsequently to the British era obtained the appellation of Romald's or Rombald's Moor, from the name of its early proprietor; but the lands to the south have been gradually enclosed, thus separating the common of Baildon from the more extensive wastes northward. . . . From the moors there is a continual incline to Baildon common, which, in itself a mountain in miniature, rises from the valley of the Aire in steep cliffs, on the uppermost of which is a high, narrow level commanding an extensive range of the surrounding district.

"The position of this hill must have early attracted the attention of the Brigantes, and its name appears to be confirmatory of its having been chosen by them as a high place of sacrifice and worship or, at the least, a beacon point.

"The name of Baildon may be derived from a similar source to that from which the word Beltan in the Beltan fires comes, of which there is an account in Brand's "Antiquities," —namely, Bael or Bel, signifying fire, a flame, or the sun, and Ton, a hill; hence Beltan or Baildon may have signified merely a beacon hill, a hill of fire. But the Beltan fires were undoubtedly of sacrificial origin, and the high places were invariably chosen for their rites. This hill, of all others here the most conspicuous, would be chosen for a hill of sacrifice to Bael. . . .

"Archæologists have found much of interest on Baildon Hill."

BAILDON

Baildon was in the Angle kingdom of Deira, A.D. 550, whence came the immortal youths seen by Gregory at Rome, and has been the seat of the family of that name from before the time of King John. It has been, since the Norman conquest, a chapelry in the West Riding of Yorkshire, situated on an eminence overlooking the river Aire. It is a short ride from Leeds, and a lovely English lane leads from the station to the Angel Inn. Here we ordered a carriage and drove through the quaint old street to the old hall, which was built by a Baildon, and was probably the dower house. Not far away stands Baildon Hall, still in a good state of preservation. The large drawing-room at the left of the entrance is wainscoted with beautifully carved English oak, and the ceiling is decorated with designs from the coats of arms of Yorkshire families. At the time of the herald's visitation in 1585 Robert Baildon, who married Isabel Maude, was the head of the family.

Francis Baildon made some alterations in the hall in 1660, and the cornice of the drawing-room bears his initials.

MAP OF BAILDON COMMON, ETC.

Showing British Remains

Encampment
No 1

ILKLEY MOOR

Lanshaw Delves   Lanshaw Lass

Little Barrow & of Stones
Cairn No 1

Lanshaw Lad   Lanshaw Dam
Druidical Circle
No 6   Wondstones Castle

B U R L E Y   M O O R
Barrow
No 3
Remains of Old Road   Cairn   Barrow of Stones
No 4   Camp No 2

Camp No 3

Orson Baw

R O M B A L D S   M O O R

Long
Ridge
Hawksworth Stone

Druidical Circle
Horndiff   HAWKSWORTH MOOR
House

Intake Gate

Sheeply Hill

Sheeply Brig   Oak Wood

Fawcather

E. Birch Close

Remains of Coal Pits

Stance Gray

Pennythorn Hill
Barrow
No 10

Acwhorth Hill

BAILDON   COMMON
Old Coal Pits
Barrow No 8
Barrow   Cairns   Low Plain
No 7
Cairns   Earth works
Dobrudden
High
Plain

Roise House
Crooks

As Francis was the last of the main line to live in Baildon, and as he was a cousin of Richard Bayldon, a little sketch of his life will not be out of place, and will show the state of Bayldon, Kippax, and other Yorkshire towns in the seventeenth century.

Francis Baildon was born four months after the death of his father, in 1627, and was therefore heir to a capital messuage, or tenement, and one hundred acres of land, meadow and pasture, in Baildon. On the death of his grandfather Francis became possessed of other Baildon property,—namely, the Manor of Baildon, twenty houses, ten cottages, one water corn-mill, two hundred acres of arable land, forty acres of meadow, one hundred and fifty acres of pasture, three hundred acres of wood, two hundred acres of furze and heath (*i.e.*, the moor), and sixty-five shillings rent in Baildon, and five bovates of arable land and pasture in Shipley and the mill at Baildon Bridge. This property, as well as the house and land that belonged to William Baildon the younger, was held of the king in chief by knight service, as of the honor of Pontefract. Young Francis accordingly became a ward of the king, which meant that the king had a right to take the whole of the infant's income during his minority ; no accounts were ever rendered, and the only obligation was to bring up and educate the ward. This was bad enough in itself, but the system actually adopted by the Court of Wards made it fifty times worse. To save the trouble of collecting rents and so on, the wretched ward and his property were sold to the highest bidder, who was called his guardian, or committee. The committee paid an annual sum to the king, and then made as much profit out of it as he could. The natural consequence of this iniquitous system was that the ward was neglected, his tenants were squeezed to the utmost, and his property reduced to the most deplorable condition ; and where the minority was a large one, as in the case of Francis Baildon, he was a lucky man indeed who was not so crippled that he had to sell his ancestral acres altogether.

In 1633, accordingly, on the 2d of May, the custody and wardship of Francis were sold to one John Browne for fifty pounds, and an allowance of two pounds per annum was made out of the income of the property for his maintenance during his minority, and on the 23d of March, 1635, in consideration of twenty shillings fine, the manor and his other property was granted unto the said John Browne during the minority at a rent of twenty pounds per annum. In February, 1636, Browne assigned the wardship and manor, etc., to Francis Neville, of Chevett, County York, and in July, 1637, Neville assigned to Francis Malham, of Elslack, in Craven, who remained guardian during the remainder of the minority.

During the civil war Francis Baildon was placed by his guardian Malham in Skipton Castle, and was there during the siege. This siege lasted for three years, beginning December, 1642, and ending December 21, 1645. During this period the condition of Baildon—and doubtless the neighboring villages were no better off—was most miserable. The following account is so graphic, being written in 1631, that I insert it in full :

" The said Manor (*i.e.*, Baildon) and premises haue layne under the burden and pressure sometimes of the Late King's Army and the Souldiers belonging thereunto, and sometimes

under the Armies and the Souldiery belonging to the parliament, who have severally dampnified the Tennants and Farmours of the said Manor by Takeing or driveing away theire Cattell, seizing and distreining of theire goods, and keepeing them untill such time as the said Tennants were forced to Fyne for and redeeme the same, and likewise the said Tennants, for support and maintenance of the parliament's forces then Lyeing at Bradford under the Command of Ferdinando Late Lord Fairfax, who commanded in chiefe in those partes, were chardged and compelled to pay divers and several summes of money contribuciones and taxes by reason whereof the said Landes for the most parte Laid wast and untennanted in the beginning of theis troubles, nor could any persons be gott to hold, mannure, and occupy the said Landes without greate abatements and defalcacions of rent and payment of such taxes and assesses as might from time to time be imposed uppon or by reason of the said Land."

In 1643, Sir Henry Fowles, knight, and Captain Dent, officers of the Bradford garrison, by order of Lord Fairfax, received all the rents and profits, amounting to one hundred pounds at the least; and in 1644 and 1645, Jeremy Bower, or Captain Bower, his son, took the whole profits. Another account says, "The Manor, Tennants, and Farmours thereof were myserably vexed with the Armyes on both partes, and payde moneyes to both respectyvely for their goods and Cattle by them driven and taken Away."

Francis married Jane, the daughter of his neighbor, Sir Richard Hawksworth, of Hawksworth, knight. The marriage probably took place in 1649, as Mary, the sole issue of the marriage, was baptized at Baildon in February, 1650.

In 1660 he was one of those chosen by King Charles II. to be invested with the Order of Knight of the Royal Oak, and the value of his estate was then given at six hundred pounds per annum. The Order was afterwards abandoned, as it was feared it would tend to keep alive party strife and hatred.

Mary, the only child of Francis Baildon, was baptized in 1650. She married, when very young, Bradwardine Tindall, of Brotherton, at Hutton Pagnell, September 21, 1665. There was only one child of this marriage, Lucy, wife of Ed. Thompson, of Marston and Settrington, County York; she died in 1715. Her last descendant, and consequently the last descendant of Francis Baildon, was Lucy Sarah, only child of Admiral Frank Sotheron. She was born in 1811, married the Right Honorable Thomas Henry Sutton Sotheron-Estcourt (president of the Poor Law Board, 1858; Home Secretary, 1859), and died without issue in 1870.

1745. In this year Tindall Thompson, Esq., suffered a recovery of the Manor of Baildon and other property in Baildon and Bingley, including the right of nomination of a clerk to the curacy of the chapel of Baildon. Tindall Thompson was the third son of Edward Thompson, of Marston, Settrington, and Baildon, in the County of York, by his wife Lucy, daughter and sole heiress of Bradwardine Tindall, of Brotherton, her mother being Mary, daughter and sole heiress of Francis Baildon, of Baildon. At the time of this recovery Tindall Thompson was the only surviving son. He was born 1698 and died 1775.

Francis Baildon was in Skipton Castle during the siege 1642–45 *ex parte regis*, for which he was fined by the Parliament six hundred and sixty pounds.

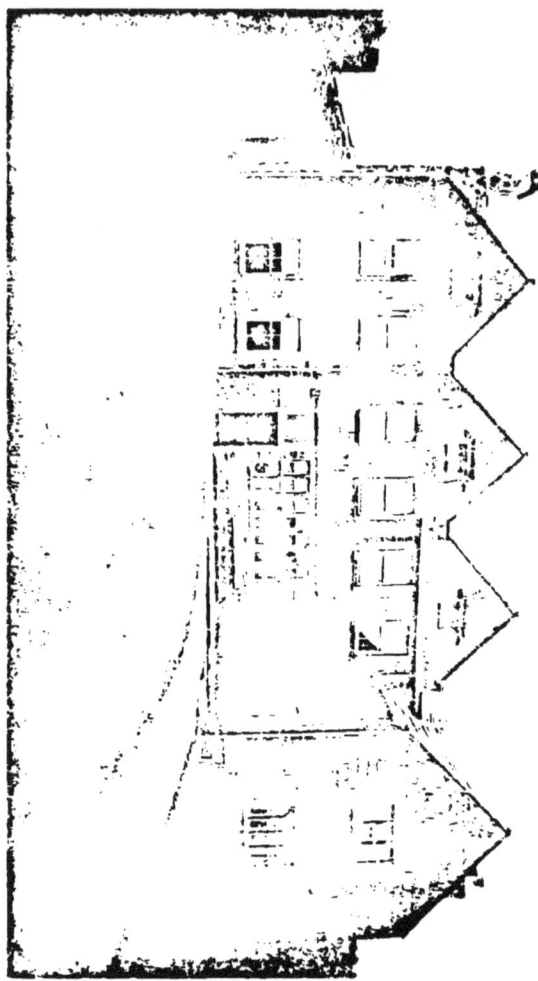

He was captain of a foot company of the trained bands in Skyrack Wapentake in 1667.

The portrait is probably by Lely, and is the property of William Paley Baildon, Esq., of London.

The advent of strangers in the village had been noised abroad, and by the time we reached the church of St. John the Evangelist a goodly company followed us at a respectful distance.

> "Nigh to a grave that was newly made
> Leaned the sexton old on his earth-worn spade."

This church is coeval with Kirkstall Abbey, and near the altar is a curiously carved old stone font. In the vestry-room is a board on which is inscribed, "This Chapel was founded by Dame Alice Quentin in the 12th Century." The next reference to this church is in 1265, when John, son of John de Baildon, Henry, the deacon of the same place, Hugh, son of Symon (de Baildon), and others, witnessed a charter dated 1265, by which Hugh de Neirford gave lands in Baildon to William the Forrester of Baildon.

In the year 1338 the venerable father in God, William de Melton, Archbishop of York, of his favor and devotion, contributed to the fabric of the church at Baildon six hundred marks of silver in aid thereof; the memorial of which (*i.e.*, the chapel) will remain throughout the ages. It would appear from this that the chapel was rebuilt in 1338, but the memorial of the archbishop's munificence did not last much over two hundred years, as we shall see later. It is not unlikely that the chapel was destroyed by the Scots. After the battle of Bannockburn, as Mr. Horsfall Turner tells us in his

23

charming "History of Ilkley," "the Scots came trooping over the border in great force, and paid us back in our own coin, for injuries we had inflicted on them in times gone by. In the summer of 1316 they burnt North Allerton, Borough-bridge, Knaresborough, and Skipton, and made such havoc in Archbishop Melton's Manor of Otley that he cursed them with bell, book, and candle." They came again three or four years after, and went over about the same ground. Baildon, being close to Otley, and, indeed, within that parish, would be sure to come in for a share of the trouble, so the chapel was probably destroyed by the Scots, and rebuilt in 1338.

1535–36. In 27 Henry VIII. we find the following description :

"The Chauntry of St. John the Evangelist in Chappell of Bayldowne, distant 4 Miles from the Parish Church. Richard Cowdrey Incumbent.

NO FOUNDATION.

But by the Benevolence of the Inhabitants of Bayldon, which is distant from the Church 4 miles. And the said Priest his Lands bought him by the Inhabitants, but hath no Evydence, for that the said Chappel was burnt as they upon ther Othes have alledg'd, Valet de Claro.

Goods and Plate.
55s. 4d.

31. 12s. 6d."

From this we see that the local tradition is perfectly correct, as it often is,—namely, that the church was burnt down in the reign of Henry VIII. The stone over the vestry door bearing the date 1549 (Cudworth's "Round About Bradford") probably gives the date of the rebuilding.

1548. In this year Edith Baildon, daughter of John Baildon, of Baildon, bequeathed her " bodie to be buried within the Chapell of Sainte John Evangeliste at Baildon." She also bequeathed to her "gostelie father, Sir Richard Cawdroe," three shillings and fourpence. He was the incumbent in 1535 and in 1549.

In the centre of the village is an old cross, and here the people of the village assembled to celebrate the Queen's Jubilee in June, 1897.

William Baildon, of Baildon (son and heir of Robert by Isabel, daughter of Thomas Maude, of West Riddlesden), was born in 1562. In 1619, Roger Dodsworth writes, " Mr' Baildon liveth at Baildon as his ancestors of long time have done in good repute."

He married, first, Margaret, daughter of Arthur Maude, of West Riddlesden (by whom he had William and John); secondly, Anne, widow of —— Haydock; thirdly, Jane, widow of Thomas Saville, of Kexborough, whose daughter Frances married William's eldest son, William.

William Baildon died intestate December 20, 1628.

The portrait is probably by Cornelius Jansen van Keulen, and is in the possession of William Paley Baildon, Esq., of London.

MUSTERS IN SKYRACK WAPENTAKE, 1539

CONTRIBUTED BY MR. W. PALEY BAILDON

" Musterys takyn at Wyke, the XXVjth day of (March) in the XXXty yere of the Reign of Oure S(overeign) Lorde Kyng Henry the VIIjth byfore Sir William (Gascoigne) th'

25

elder, Sir William Myddilton, and Sir William Maleuerer, knyghtes, assyned and allotyd by devysion to the Wapentak of Skyrak, w'in yᵉ liberty and w'out in ye Westr' of ye countie of Yorke, by vertue of the Kynge's Gracius (?) comyssion to theym and other derectyd for ye same Musters.

(Signed)   " WYLLM GASCOYGNE, k.

" WYLLM MYDDYLLTON, k.

" WYLLM MALEUERER, k."

THE TOWNSHIP OF BAYLDON

" Thes be archers, horsed and harnessed, abill persons :

  " ROBERT BAYLDON, gentylman,

  " EDWARD WATTERHOUSE,

  " THOMAS BYSTON.

" Thes be billmen parcell harnessed, abill persons :

  " WILLIAM STEDE ; jak and salet.

  " RYCHERD BAILY ; jake.

  " RICHERD YLLYNGWORTH ; a salet.

  " THOMAS LYSTER ; a horse.

" Thes be archers havying no harnez, abill persons, footmen :

  " ROBERT TAYLLOR,

  " WILLIAM HUDSON,

  " THOMAS BYSTON,

  " DANELL OBSON,

  " WILLIAM WTYD,

  " LEONERD STEDE,

  " RICHARD WAYTE.

INTERIOR OF BAILDON HALL
1897

"Thes be bilmen havyng no harnes; abill persons, footmen:

"GYLS HARTLE (Hartley)
"JAMES TOMLYNGSON,
"WILLIAM OBSON,
"RICHARD LYSTER,
"JOHN STEDE."

Mauger de Baildon was prior of the Order of St. Mary of Mount Carmel, York, in 1387.

There was a Richard Bayldon in 1399.

Henry Baildon was master of the Hospital of St. Thomas the Martyr at Bolton in 1433.

Adam de Baildon was vicar of Gedyngham before 1392.

METHLEY PARK

The seat of the Earl of Mexborough is still occupied by the Saviles. The back of the hall was probably built by Sir John Savile in 1593. The front was built about the beginning of this century. It was famous for a vast gallery, in the window of which the arms of the Yorkshire families were arranged in wapentakes. Frances Savile married William Baildon, of Baildon.

This window is still in Methley Hall.

KIPPAX

Kippax, the home of Sir Francis Bayldon, is in the West Riding of Yorkshire, not far from Baildon. We drove from the station through the lovely old village to Kippax Hall, a stately mansion, built within the last hundred years. It is on the site of the old hall, and from its windows is an unobstructed view of forty miles of rolling country.

At the church we were met by the vicar, the Rev. E. B. Smith, who had previously searched the registers for us, and who with justifiable pride called our attention to the well-kept church-yard and the renovation of the interior of the church.

As all Baildon and Kippax records had been collected before our arrival, we spent only a few hours at Kippax, and after tea at the Royal Oak took the train for Leeds.

SIR FRANCIS BAYLDON

(REEVE OF KIPPAX)

Francis Bayldon, who built the hall at Kippax, was of the Bayldons of Bayldon, and was born in 1560. He was the son of George Bayldon, and married, first, Frances, daughter and co-heir of Henry Johnson, of Leathley; she was buried at Kippax, May 21, 1587. His second wife was Margaret, daughter of Richard Goodrick, of Ribston; she was buried September 22, 1598.

Francis, the eldest son, was by the first wife, and there were eight children by the second wife, Margaret Goodrick,—William, Richard, Cuthbert, Martin, Henry, Thomas, Muriell, and Clare.

Francis Bayldon was knighted at Whitehall, at the coronation of the king, July 23, 1603.

At that time the qualifications for knighthood were such that no trader could be created, nor any one of a servile con-

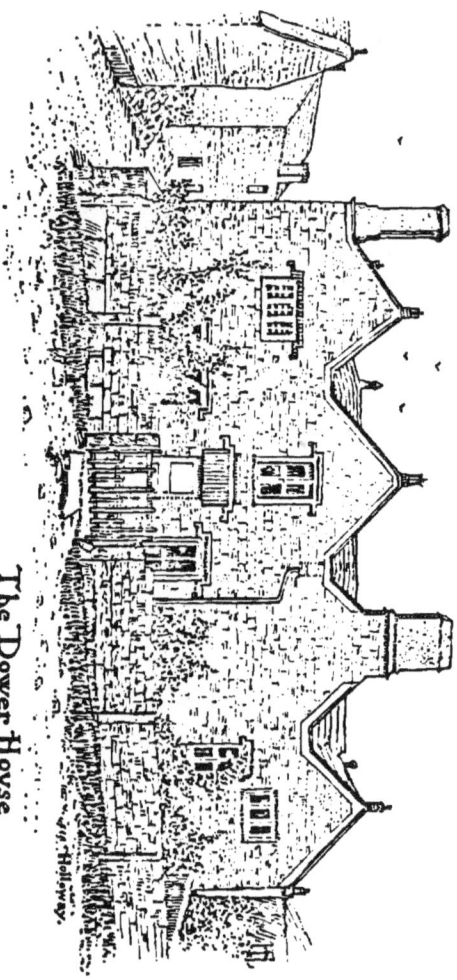

The Dower House
Baildon

dition. It was then requisite that he should be brave, expert, well-behaved, and of good morals. A candidate being approved of, he presented himself at the church, confessed his sins, had absolution given him ; he heard mass, watched his arms all night, placed his sword on the altar, which was returned by the priest, who gave him his benediction; the sacrament was administered to him, and, having bathed, he was dressed in rich robes, and his spurs and sword put on. He then appeared before his chief, who dubbed him knight. The ceremony then concluded with feasting and rejoicing.

Knighthood is not hereditary, but acquired. It does not come into the world with a man, like nobility, nor can it be revoked. It was anciently the custom to knight every man of rank and fortune, that he might be qualified to give challenges, to fight in the lists, and to perform feats of arms. The sons of kings and kings themselves, with all other sovereigns, in former days had knighthood conferred upon them as a mark of honor. They were usually knighted at their baptism or marriage, at their coronation or before battle.

Sir Francis Bayldon's third wife was Isabel, daughter of Sir Philip Tyrwhit; she was buried March 9, 1610.

He married for the fourth time, Anne Coleby, who, after his death, in 1623, was in constant litigation with the other heirs until 1628, when the estate was finally settled. In the early part of the seventeenth century the Bayldons, like other families, was broken up into several branches. Younger sons in those days had not much chance unless (like George Bayldon, of Kippax) they made a good marriage, or were phenomenally successful in law, the church, or commerce.

Sir Francis of Kippax was a man of large property. His

estate was somewhat involved and some of his investments were of a highly speculative nature. Still, even his younger sons must have found themselves in the possession of a considerable sum of money when their father's estate was finally wound up.

As the only Wethersfield in England is not far from Hatfield, the home at that time of Sir Thomas Barrington, who was colonel of the company of which Martin, Richard's brother, was major, it is not unlikely that Richard, after the division of his father's property, joined one of the expeditions fitted out by Sir Thomas for America.

It is known that Sir Thomas corresponded with Sir Richard Saltonstall, John Masters, and George Minott.

OFFICIAL RECORDS

" *The Queen,* etc, Greeting. *Whereas* by our Letters Patent dated at Westminster July 28 A o 13, 1571, made to Robert Yaxley, reciting that by Letters Patent dated at Westminster Feb. 17 A o 3. 1561, we leased to William Tyndall, gentleman, the titles of grain arising in the town and field of Kepax co. York, together with the title barn, and a croft or parcel of land adjoining, previously demised to Robert Chaloner, esquire deceased, parcel of the Rectory of Kepax, lately belonging to the Monastery of Pontefract, reserving all great trees, woods, underwoods, minerals and quarries, to hold to Tyndall, his executors and assigns from Michaelmas last (1560) for 21 years at a rent of £7—6—8, And by the said first named Letters Patent we granted the said titles to Yaxley, from Michaelmas 1581, for 21 years, at

CHURCH OF S. JOHN THE EVANGELIST, BAILDON

(see page 3)

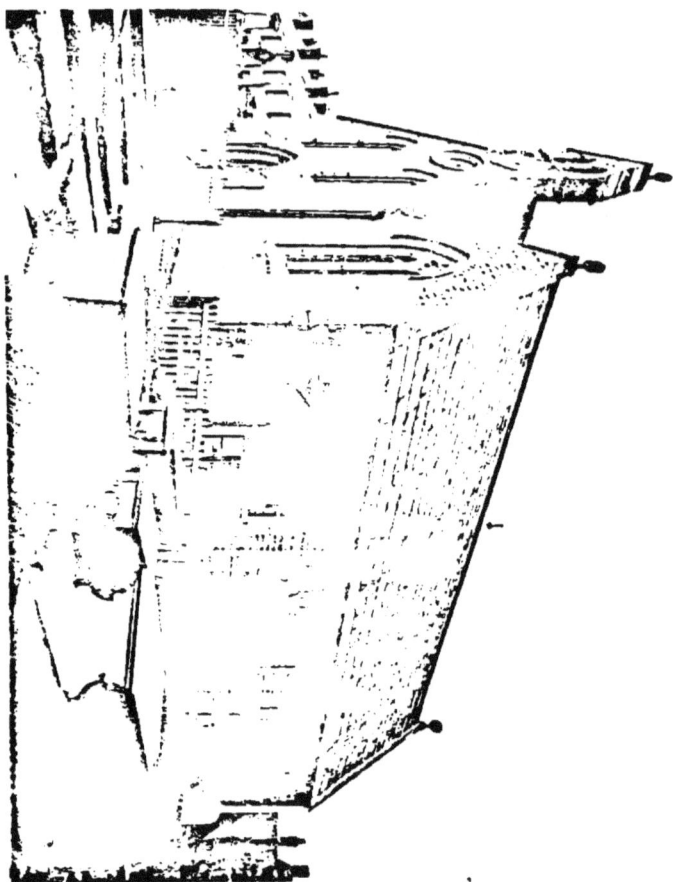

the same time rent; *And whereas* all Yaxley's interest in the
said term of years is now belonging to Francis Bayldon, gentleman, who has surrendered the same to us, *We*, in consideration of a fine of £7, 6s., 8d do hereby lease to Francis
Bayldon, Margaret his wife and William their son *All* the
said titles of grain in Kepax together with the title barn and
the croft, *to hold* To Francis Bayldon for life, and after his
decease, surrender or forfeiture, to Margaret Baildon for life,
and after her decease surrender or forfeiture, to William
Bayldon and his assigns for life, at a rent of £7, 6s., 8d, and
also paying £3 by way of a heriot on the death of either of
them. The lessees are to keep the barn in repair. Dated at
Kewe July 12th A o 35, 1593."

Chancery Enrolled Decrees, Eliz. Roll 57, *No.* 13.

1584. "Where Fraunces Bayldon of Walton Heade in the
Countye of Yorke gent. hathe exhibited his bill of Com-
plainte into this honorable Courte of Chauncerye againste
Richarde Goldesboroughe, Esquier, and others, defendantes,
Declaringe by the same that where one Henrye Johnson
Esquier late of Walton Heade aforesaide, Father's in Lawe
unto the saide Complaynaute, was aboute eightene yeres laste
paste, and lawfullye seised in his demeane as of feeof and
upon the Mannors or lordeshipps of Walton Heade, Fearne-
ley and Leathley in the saide Countye of Yorke, amongeste
other thinges beinge parcell of his inheritaunce and he soe
beinge thereof seised did by his indenture of lease aboute the
same tyme sufficiente in the lawe demyse, graunte, and to
ferme lette all the saide severall Mannors or lordeshipps
amongeste other thinges, unto one Edmonde Norton, then of

Rawclyffe, gent., and brother in lawe unto the saide Henrye
Johnson, for the terme of 60 yeres yf he, the saide Henrye
Johnson shoulde soe longe fortune to lyve, the whiche lease
was onlye mente and soe made upon tryste and confidence
and to th' intente that the said Norton, his executors admyn-
istrators and assignes, shoulde have and enioye the same
Mannors and premisses to the use of him the saide Johnson,
Elizabeth his wife, and Elizabethe, Frances and Suzan chil-
drene of the saide Johnson, then beinge infantes of verye tender age (that Norton assigned the trust to William Burnandl
of Yorke Esquier, who about five years ago conveyed the same
to the defendant Richard Goldesbrughe, who had married
Elizabeth, one of the daughters of the said Henry Johnson)
sythence whiche tyme the complaynante had married and
taken to wyfe the said Frances one other of the daughters of
the saide Henrye Johnston,   And that by reason thereof not
onelye one fourthe part of the premisses oughte to be assured
to the Complaynante by vertue of the saide truste, but also the
fourth parte of the proffittes thereof oughte to be answered
to the said plaintyffe whiche hathe bene alreadye receyued.
And further by his said bill alledged that one Will'm Justice
maryed Suzan, one other of the daughter of the saide Johnson, whoe sythence his saide entermaryage had by good and
sufficiente conveyaunce aboute twoe yeres sythence conveyed
to the Complaynante his purparte, estate, righte, title, interest
and terme of and in the said Mannors and premisses whiche
did or shoulde belonge unto the said Justyce and Suzan his
wyfe in the righte of the same Suzane by vertue of the said
recyted demyse, for the terme of XXI yeres then nexte fol-
louringe, whereby the said Complaynante oughte to have and

STATION AND POST-OFFICE, BAILDON, 1897

From photographs taken by M. Van Z. Belden

enioye twoe partes of all the said recyted premisses, beinge
the halfe of the whole for XXI yeres from the tyme of the
said assuraunce made by the said Justice, and one fourth
parte for and duringe the whole terme of 60 yeres yf the said
Johnson shall so longe fortune to lyve,   And the Complaynante declared and would be ready to prove that Henry Johnson ys yet lyvinge at Walton Heade aforesaid   And further
declared that the originall lease made by Johnson to Norton
was by casuall meanes comen into t' handes and custodye and
possession of the Defendant whoe by color of havinge thereof
had wrongfullye entered into the said moytye of the said
Mannors or lordshipps, the halfe whereof of righte belonginge
to the Complaynante

"And thereof or of a great parte thereof had dispossessed
the Complaynante; And further declared that whereas the
said Complaynante occcupied a parcell of the said Mannor
of Walton Heade, the said Defendante Goldesborough of his
like wronge did dayly threaten to expell and remove him out
of the same, (Goldesborough had always refused to assure
the moity of the said Mannors to the plaintiff or to account
for the half profits, etc.)

"And the said Goldesboroughe for answere alledged and
confessinge the said Henrye Johnson to be seised of the
premisses amongest other thinges, and beinge geven to un-
thryftynes and excess yne expences and havinge throughe
occasion thereof solde and consumed a greate parte of his in-
herytaunce absolutlye awaye from him and his heyers entered into a bargen and sale of certen landes and tenementes
called Tranmere and Olde Hall lyeinge in the said Countye
of Yorke to one Will'm Hawkesworth esquier, which landes

were parcell of the jointure of Elizabeth Johnson wyfe of
Henrye, for the perfectinge of which sale Elizabeth was to
joyne in a fyne with Henrye for the clere passinge awaye
thereof and to avoid and barre her for havinge any interest
or dower therin after his decease yf she did survive him, and
therupon Henrye required her to joyne with him in the
said fyne, which she refused to doe unles Henrye woulde be
contented to assure the resydue of all his Mannors, etc,
whiche were by him graunted and conveyed to certen persons
for the joynture of Elizabeth, to such person or persons as
she should nominate, for suche nomber of yeres as Johnson
should lyve, to th' entents he should have now power to dispose or medle therewith all duringe his lyfe, whiche he was
contented to assure accordinglye, and did geve his faythfull
promise to Master Justice Welshe and Master Seriaunt Pow-
trell, then Justices of Assyse to make the said assurance
accordinglye upon which promise the said Elizabethe joyned
with Henrye in the fyne to Hawkesworthe, and afterwards
in performance of his promise did by his Indenture of lease
demise unto the said Edmond Norton amongste other thinges
all that his Mannor of Leatheley, etc., and all the Lordshippe of Famely, etc., and all the Mannor of Lordshippe of
Walton Heade, etc., To have and to holde from the daye of
the date thereof for 60 yeres yf Johnson so longe did lyve,
payeinge yerelye therefore one Redd Rose at the Feaste
of St John Baptyste yf it were lawefully asked,   By vertue
wherof Norton became possessed thereof,   And Norton
beinge so possessed Johnson did enter into the late actuall
Rebellyon in the North partes and thereof was atteynted of
Highe treason,   After which one Will'm Knype supposinge

MARKET-PLACE, BAILDON

Decorated for the Queen's Jubilee, June. 1897

that the premisses were come to the Quene's maiesties handes
did procure twoe leases of the same to him for the terme of
diuers yeres, and therupon did commence sute againste Norton and others for the said Mannors or a greate parte thereof
in the Courte of Exchequer at Westm'   And that after
Norton did graunte unto Will'm Byrhande of Howden co
Yorke Esquier, deceased, all his interest in the said Indenture of lease made by Johnson, Byrhande not havinge, to the
defendantes knowledge anye notice of anye use lymyted to
any person or persons named in the bill, and that Birnand
beinge thereof soe possessed, the said Elizabeth Johnson declared to the defendante that she was doutefull leste Birnand
beinge learned in the lawes and one who was greatly busyed
with his clyentes causes that he could not have tyme to
defend the title againste Knype, and declared likewyse that
she had receyued of the tennantes and fermers of the premisses diuer sommes of money and promised them therfore to
procure them leases of their tenementes for certen yeres, and
had likewyse borrowed diuers great sommes of moneye for
the defence of the lease, and for the discharge of the same
sommes and for the better defence of the lease, she willed the
deft. to take an assignment of the lease from Byrnand, and
that after he would make leases to the tenantes, and paye the
money borrowed by Elizabeth, and allowe unto her some
thinge for her mayntenance and staye of lyvinge and that he
would disburse some moneye for the charges of the pardon
of the said Johnson before that tyme obteyned,   All which
the def. was contented to do, and therupon Byrnand did
assigne to the def. all his interest in the said Mannor, etc.,
And that afterwards the def. did become bounden by Recog-

nizaunce in the somme of £400 with condicion that he should paye £200 which was spente in defence of the title of the saide lease, After which Knype and others did commence sute against the def. for the premises as well at Yorke before the Counsell there as elsewhere, and that by meanes thereof the defendante was put to greate and excessyue charges so that he was forced to let the premisses And therupon in consideracion of diuers sommes of money payed by the auncyent tenantes and Fermors of the said Mannors, and by others, did by his severall leases demise and let all the said Mannors savinge certen parcells thereof of a smale value, to the said tenantes and others for the terme of diuers yeres yet enduringe And further that Knype prosecuted his sute in the Exchequer and broughte the same to tryall at the Guilde Hall in London before Sir Roger Manwood Knighte Lord Chiefe baron of the Exchequer. And the verydytte passed for the def. and the other persons againste Knype And further alledged that by meanes of the sutes, etc., he had disbursed the somme of £900, And further that the Complaynante (dependinge this sute) hath conveyed his interest to one Richarde Goodericke, esquier, so that the compl. had not anye tytle therein. And further trauersed the reste of the Bill

"Alexander Ingle, Xpofer Harryson, Laurence Harryson, and Henrye Thorneton, foure other defendantes, likewyse made answere alledginge somme mysdemenors practised by the plaintyf and for those parcells of grounde in their severall occupacions, they helde the same by lease from Goldesboroue, and had payed greate sommes of moneye for the same

"Unto which answers the plaintyf replyed and the def. Goldesboroughe reioyned

THE OLD HALL.

Erected Sixteenth Century: demolished about 1808. (See page 59)

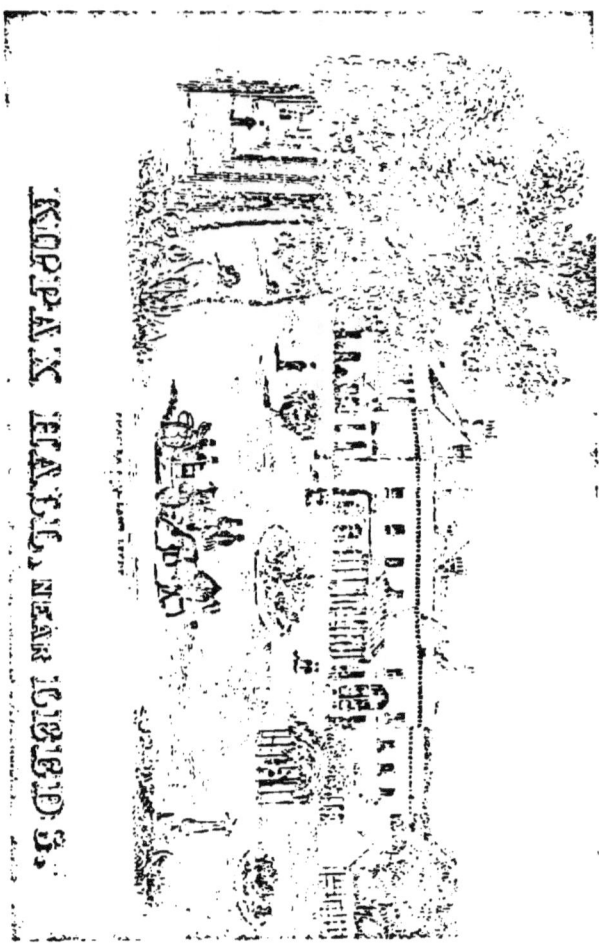
KOPAX HALL, NEAR LEEDS.

"And afterwardes about the XXVIII of December laste paste as well Francis Bayldon the compl., and Richarde Gooderick and Will'm Justice of th' one parte and Richard Goldesboroughe of the other parte did submitte themselves to the awarde and fynall determynacion of John Norton, Richard Allbroughe and Will'm Malyuerer, Esquiers, and Francis Tanckarde, gent., arbytrators chosen by them to arbytrate and fynally determyne all sutes variaunces and troubles amongst the said parties, And that yf there were noe awarde made by the arbytrators before a certen daye, then the parties did submytte themselves to th' award and unperage of the righte Honorable Henry, Earle of Huntingdon. And for the better performance of the said award, Gooderick, Bayldon & Justice are bounde by seuerall oblygacions unto Goldesboroughe in seuerall somes of moneye and Goldesboroughe is like wyse bounde to them for the performaunce of the award, which said arbytrators did make no award before the said daye, for which cause the Earle, havinge had all the parties before him and havinge hard their demaundes did make his awarde which beareth date the XXIIIth daye of Maye laste paste, upon which award the quene's Solicitor generall upon Wednesdaye the firste of Julye laste moved to have a subpena against the def. to showe cause whie th' award made by the Earle of Hunttingdon by consente of both parties should not be decreed, and on the morowe the IInd of Julye, the said master solicitor generall on the behalfe of the plaintyf alledged that in the awarde there was incerted a clause that the plaintyf should not sue the def. for any matter conteyned therein, and therefore the Solycitor coulde noe further make sute to have the awarde decreed, but made humble sute that the whole cause in question might be dismyssed.

"It is therfore this presente terme of the Hollye Trynitie, that is to saye, the IInd daye of Julye in the XXVIth yere of the raigne of our Soueraigne Ladye Elizabethe etc. By Sir Thomas Bramley, Knighte, Lord Chauncellor ordered adjudged and decreed that as well the said plaintyfe as the defendant together with the cause in question in this Courte be from hence fullye clerelye and absolutelye dismyssed."

Decree Roll 241, *No.* 3.

"The plaintiff by his Bill declaring that Sir Edward Tirwhitt, Sir Jervise Clifton, Sir John Molineux and Sir Francis Baildon by Indenture dated July 6, 13 James I (1615) demised to Thomas Whaley and Cuthbert Baildon the Manors of Ircforth alias Arforth and Sotherey alias Sency Place Lincolnshire and also the site of the Monastery of Irforth, and a messuage and lands in Caborne, Co. Lincoln to hold after the dertermination of some estates for lives to Sir Philip Tirwhitt and Dame Martha his wife, for 99 years at a rent of 12d and that the lease was made by the special direction of Sir Francis for the benefit of Cuthbert, and that it was made by Tirwhitt to secure to Sir Francis the payment of £1100 and interest at £8 per cent, and Sir Edwards entered into a Recognizance to perform the same and to free Sir Francis from all obligations as he was then bound in for Sir Edward. Sir Edward did not pay the £1100 nor free Sir Francis from the said obligations though the same were very great, about Nov. 1, 13 James I 1615, Sir Francis made his will, (as set out elsewhere), Henry and Thomas Baildon died

38

MOULDING FROM OLD HALL, KIPPAX

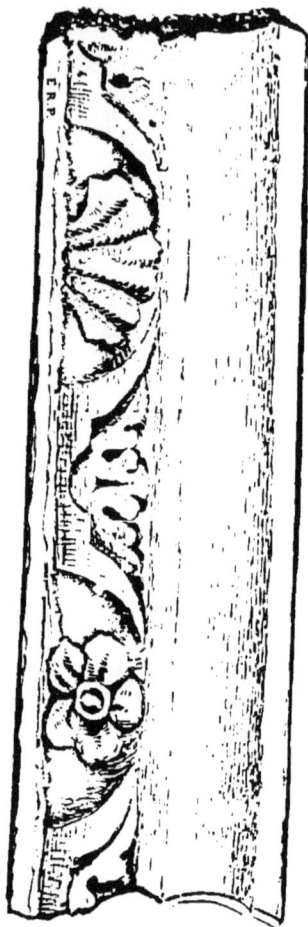

in the lifetime of Sir Francis so that the residue of the said £1100 accrued to Cuthbert, Richard and Martin. On Dec. 8, 1615, Thomas Colby and the Plaintiff by the appointment of Sir Francis, did assign their interest in the said lands to Sir Thomas Dawnay, Sir Henry Goodrick and John Colby in trust to enable them to perform the declarations of Sir Francis, he died in June 1622; John Colby and Thomas Colby are also dead ——

"Ordered May 5, 1627, that Sir Thomas Dawney shall upon request release his interest in the said Manor of Irforth and the other premises limitted by the will to be sold, to Sir Henry Goodrick, and that Sir Henry shall sell the same, and that they shall both then be discharged from the said trust, Sir Edward Tirwhitt shall have the refusal of the property at its market value, the purchase money to be distributed according to the will."

The recognizance was for four thousand pounds.

Close Roll, 13 Jac. I., Part 42, No. 94.

Meriall Chatterton wife of Edmond Chatterton of Milforth gentl. aged 24 years saith that hir father Sr Francis Baildon did take diuerse bonds in hir name and that she thinketh some of them weare dischardged before his death but shee further saith that theare weare certayn bonds taken in hir name & left for hir porcion of w'ch shee and hir husband Mr Chatterton hath received CCIX li. That besides the CCIX li hir husband hath Received from Mr Colby about xpmas last lvj li vj s viij d towards hir porcion appointed by hir Father in his will

"That this examinate & hir husband about xpmas last did

deliver seale and subscribe their names to a writing made to xpofer Colby w'ch shee thinketh was a releas of such interest as shee and her husband might clayme to the lands of Sr Edward Tirwhitt That she hath heard Sr Francis Baildon oftentimes say w'th much grief and sorow of heart that Sr Edward Tirwhitt had undonn him and his children, and his disbursm'tes and engagem'tes for Sr Edward did amount to £2000 and more.

" *Cuthbert Bramham*, of Kippax, aged 30 yeares, saith he hath very often heard Sr Francis complayne that he was out of purse & engaged for Sr Edward Tirwhitt £2700; and that, he being his servant and wayting uppon him in London, Sr Francis durst not walke abroade but kept his house for feare to be arrested for the said engagm'tes; and that Sr Francis was diverse times arrested for the detts of Sr Edward, as namely by one, Mr. Smyth, a Scrivener dwelling in Cornwall,* London, for £100 w'ch he paid, and by one Mr. Blake, a Scrivener in London, for £120 w'ch he paid likewise, and for £100 by one Mr. Day, an Ironmunger in graciouse† street London w'ch he paid and likewise for LX li to one Will'm Yutter a scrivenor in London w'ch likewise he paid and likewise to one Mr. Peacocke a merchant of London LX li and to one Mr. Besta Scrivenor in London a C li all w'ch was for the dett of Sr Edward besids other small debtes all w'ch premisses he cann confidently depose in respect he paid the money or carryed the same to be paid and that Sr Francis Baildon being at London diuerse times removed his lodging for feare to be arrested.

---

* Cornhill.   † Gracechurch Street.

KIPPAX HALL, 1897

Erected about 1800

KIPPAX HALL

Rear View

"Thomas Bywater of Hillam aged 43 yeares saith that he
and one John Hemingway wear bound to Miss Merriall
Baildon in a bond of LX li for payment of XXIX li VIJ s.
to Merriall w'ch he hath paid to Mr. Chatterton her husband
and hath an acquittance & X li to Sr Francis in his lifetime."

Close Roll, 45 *Eliz.*, *Part* 4, 1602.

"Indenture made 4th Sept 44 Eliz 1602 between Richard
Goldesbrough of Waltonhead Co York, Esq of the one part,
and Francis Bayldon of Kypax, gentleman of the other part.
Whereas Thomas Goldesbrough of G deceased father of
Richard by an Indenture dated Nov. 8, 1556 demised to
Nicholas Savile of Newhall nigh Eland, Esq. and his heirs
and assigns for ever, the manor of Kexbrough with appurtenances in the parishes of Durton and Cawthorne and all
his property in Kexbrough Durton and Cawthorne at a rent
of £11 payable at 'the font stone of the parishe Churche of
Goldesbrough' Richard G. is now owner of the said rent; in
consideration of £21 he assigns the said rent to Bayldon
after the death of Cicily wife of John Emot of Farnham,
Clerk, proviso for repayment within five years."

1602. "Indenture dated Sept. 4th 44 Elizabeth 1602 Between Richard Goldesborough of Waltonheade Esq. of the
one part and Francis Bayldon of Kippax gentleman of the
other part Whereas Thomas Goldesbrough of G. Esq. deceased father of Richard by Indenture dated Nov. 8th 3 and 4
Philip and Mary 1556 did lease unto Nicholas Savile of Newhall near Eland, Esq., deceased, his heirs and assigns forever
the Mannor of Kexbrough with divers messuages and lands in

K. and in the parishes of Darton and Cawthorne, paying therefore yearly a fee farm rent of £11 which said rent has now come unto the said Richard.

"It was witnessed that in consideration of £21 Goldesbrough conveyed to Bayldon All the said rent of £11 to hold unto and to the use of Bayldon his heirs and assigns immediately after the death of Cicily wife of John Emott of Farnham, Clerk Covenants: for good right to convey, freedom from incumbrances, for further assurance during the next six years. Proviso for redemption on payment of £21 by Goldesborough his heirs or assigns within five years next at the 'newe dwellinge house of the said Francis Bayldon in Kippax.'"

Close Roll, 4 James I., Part 40.

1607. February 7. "Francis Bayldon of Bligthborowe Suffolk, Knight, was bound to the Lord Chancellor and the Master of the Rolls in £40, on condition that Sir Francis shall observe the terms of an order of the Court of Chancery made Nov. 28th last in a suit between himself as plaintiff and Henry Churche defendant.

Close Roll, to James I., Part 8, No. 15.

1608. "Indenture dated 12 June to James I 1608 between Grace Claxon, Widow, of Sainte Bottolphes parishe in Thomas Streete London, one of the daughters of John Liversedge of Drighlinton, co. York, and only sister to Robert Liversedge, son of the said John of the one part, and Sir Francis Bayldon Knight of the other part; Bargain and Sale to Sir Francis of a messuage and appurtenances in the lordships and parishes of Swillington and Kippax, Co. York, which is men-

KIPPAX CHURCH

Believed to date from the Norman period. Drawn from photographs taken by M. Van Z. Belden

Kippax Church
and
Churchyard

Kippax
Church

tioned in a pair of Indentures, dated 13th June 16 Elizabeth 1574, o.e., with a croft called Killinge Croft on the last of the said messuage, 2 acres of arable land called Cawdacle Hill 2 acres in the Morefeilde, 3 acres in the Kirkfield at Swillington, and an acre, containing 6 lands; in Sleginberye brigge feilde alias Berkfield, by which Indentures the said John Liversedge the father, covenanted to stand seised to the use of himself for life, remainder to his wife (if any) for life, remainder to Robert his son and his heirs for ever. To Hold unto and to the use of the use of Sir Francis, his heirs and assigns for ever."

Close Roll, 14 *James I., Part* 17, *No.* 33.

1616. May 16. " Indenture made between Sir Francis Baildon of Kipax, Knight, Thomas Rookewood of London, Esq., and Edward Rowlte of Graves Inn, Esq., of the one part, and Sir William Smith of Hammersmith, Knight of the other part Reciting the conveyance of the Manor or lordship of Wensleydale, etc by Ludoric Duke of Lennox to the parties of the first part at the request of Sir John Throckmorton John Colby, Samuel Hales and Henry Goodrick and in consideration of £10,000 by Indenture dated August 7, 1614 and reciting an Indenture of the same date, declaring the trusts of the before recited Indenture, r. a. that Throckmorton & Colby were each to have one third and Hales and Goodrick one third between them. Throckmorton having sold his third to Sir William Smith for £800, and Smith having sold half the said third to the Goodmans Baildon and the others now convey to Smith at his request the remaining half of the one third."

Ancestors and Descendants of

CUTHBERT BAYLDON,

brother of Richard, was lieutenant of the Sixty-seventh Troop of Horse, of which Oliver Cromwell was captain.

"Cromwell already knew in his own person wherein lay the strength of Puritanism and the secret of its success. 'To match men of honor,' he said, 'they must have men with the fear of God before them and would make some conscience of what they did.'

"On this principle of selection he enlisted around him a regiment of one thousand men, whose title of Ironsides has become famous in history. *They were never beaten."—En-cyclopædia Britannica.*

Chancery B. and A., Charles I., B. 135, No. 28.

"24 Jan. 1626

"Humbly sheweth yo'r Oratour Cuthbert Baildon gent. one of the sounes of Sr Francis Baildon late of Kippax knight deceased That whereas Sr Edward Tirwhitt knight Sr Jervase Clifton knight and Barronett Sir John Mollineux knight and Barronett and the said Sr Francis Baildon by Indenture bearing date the sixt daie of July 1615 13 James I did demise unto Thomas Colbye Cittizen and Grocer of London and to yo'r said Oratour the Mannors of Irforth alias Urforth and Sotherey alias Senay place in the County of Lincolne and the scite and demeasnes of the late dissolved Monasterie of Irforth alias Urforth and one Messuage and Twentie-six Acres of land meaddowe and pasture thereunto belonging and Common of pasture for 600 sheepe in Caborne in the said Countie: To have and to hould (from and after

44

CHARTER OF ABOUT THE YEAR 1195.

Probably the earliest extant instance of the use of the surname of Baildon

P. 2.

the surrender of other determinacion of some severall estates
for life or lives then formerly made of the premisses to Sr
Philip Tirwhitt, knight and Barronett, and to Dame Martha
his wife) for the tearme of 99 years by the yearely Rent of
12d w'th other covenants therein Contained w'ch said Indenture of demise was made by the speciall direccion of the said
Sr Francis Baildon for the benefit of yo'r said Orator whome
hee intended thereby to advance.   And the said demise was
soe made by Sr Edward Tirwhitt for securitie to yo'r Orators
said father of payment of £1100 w'th Interest after the Rate
of Eight pounds in the hundred upon the Feast Daie of St
Michaell Th'archangell 1617   And for the securitie of free-
ing Sr Franc's Baildon his heires executors and administrators from all such obligacions as the said Sr Francis then
stoode bound in w'th and for Sr Edward.   And for the
proper debts of Sr Edward.   And Sr Edward Tirwhitt became bound to Sr Francis Baildon by Statute or Recognizance in a great penalty defeazanced to performe the Covenants in the said first-recited Indenture contayned.   As by
certaine Indentures of defeazance made betweene the said
parties if yoor Orator had the same to shewe would alsoe appeare   And the said Sr Edward Tirwhitt did not paie the
said £1100 nor any part thereof at the time lymited or at
any time sithence neither did discharge yo'r Orators Father
from all or any the obligacions wherein yo'r Orators Father
stoode then engaged for the said Sr Edward Tirwhitt   And
by reason of default of payment of the said £1100 and dis-
engagem'ts as aforesaid the said Thomas Colbye and yo'r
Orator were lawfully possessed of the Reuercion of the said
Mannors and premisses for the said tearme of 99 years   And

45

afterwards about the fift daie of November 13 James I Sr Francis Baildon, with the consent of yo'r Orator, and upon the faithfull promise of the said Sr Francis that he would otherwise recompence yo'r said orator, did make his last Will and Testament, and thereby did declare That if the said Sr Edward Tirwhitt or his heires should be readie and willing to paie the said £1100 at the day appointed for payment thereof according to the said Indenture of Defeazance, that then he should pay the somme of £1000 and no more together with the Interest of the same, and th' other £100 Sr Francis Baildon did then forgive, And he did will that the said £1000 should be disposed of as vizt., First whereas the said Sr Francis Baildon did intend to his daughter Meriall Baildon 500 li or more for hir porcion and had then formerly taken certaine bonds in hir name, his will was that soe much of the said £1000 as would (w'th the principall in the said Bonds in hir name taken) make up for hir £500, to be put out for hir best use; And yo'r Orator further shewett That the principall Debts due by Bonds taken in the name of Meriall Baildon did amount to 350 li, w'th 150 li more out of the said 1000 li did amount to the said somme of 500 li intended to hir; And the said Sr Francis did appoint unto Sr Henry Goodrick knight 400 li parcell of the said £1000 in trust to be disposed of for the maintenance of Clare Kightley, then wife of Laurence Kightley, daughter of Sr Francis, and of hir children, And the rest of the said 1000 li and the whole of the interest thereof Sr Francis did devise that the same should be devided amongst his then five sonnes, Richard, Cuthbert, Martin, Henry and Thomas Baildon, w'ch said Henry and Thomas afterwards died intestate

SIGNATURE OF RICHARD BAYLDON, 1626

HUGH DE BAILDON, 1304

w'thout yssue in the life time of Sr Francis by reason whereof
the residue of the said 1000 li and the Interest doth accrue
unto yo'r Orator and to Richard and Martin Baildon his
brother. And Sr Francis Baildon did appoint that if Sr
Edward Tirwhitt or his heires should not pay the said
1000 li Then the lease should be sould by his supervizors
and the money should be disposed of by them as is before
lymmitted And did give the rest of his goods and Chattells to
Richard, Cuthbert and Martin Baildon Sr Henry Goodrick
(in trust for Clare Kightley) and Meriall Baildon equally
And Sr Francis Baildon did appoint Sr Thomas Dawney
and Sr Henry Goodrick knightes Richard Hutton then Es-
quior and St'ient at Lawe now Sr Richard Hutton knight
one of his Ma'ts Justices of the Court of Common Pleas
Thomas Wentworth and John Coleby esquiors and one Robert Houghton gent. supervisors of his will And about the
eight daie of December 1615 Thomas Coleby and yo'r Orator
did assigne all their Interest in the said Mannors etc to Sr
Thomas Dawney Sr Henry Goodrick and John Colby three
of the supervisors in order to perform the declaracions of the
said Will And about the moneth of June 20 James I 1622
Sr Francis Baildon ————— died seised and possessed of
a verie great estate reall and personall; And the said John
Colbye and Thomas Colbye are alsoe deceased And whereas
one Thomas Prine of Kippax Yoeman, and Lawrence Hutchinson of Metheley, Yeoman, were possessed for diverse yeares
then and yett to come in the Mannors and Lo'pps of Eagle
and Northstarle in the County of Lincolne, by vertue of one
Indenture of Lease made by the said Sr Edward Tirwhitt Sr
Jarvase Clifton Sir John Mollineux and Sr Francis Baildon

by the speciall direcion and in trust for Sir Francis and for his further indempnitye against the said debts and en- gagemts, All which were agreed should be fully satisfied by Sr Edward at the Feast of Saint Michaell Th' archangell, 1617, otherwise the said lease to remayne in force, The said Prince and Hutchinson being soe possessed did, by the speciall direccion of Sr Francis and for the sole benefitt of yo'r Orator and for his further advancem't, and in leiue of such parte of the said Mannors and premisses before men- cioned as were formerly assigned by yo'r Orator and the said Thomas Colbye as aforesaid, by their Indenture dated May 18, 1617, assigne to yo' Orator and to Sr Thomas Dawney and Sr Henry Goodrick in trust for yo'r Orator and for his sole benefitt, All the estate and interest of them Prince and Hutchinson in the Mannors of Eagle and Northscarle, for- merly demised as aforesaid. And yo'r Orator in the Tearme of the Holy Trinite 1 Charles , did exhibitt his Bill of Complaint into this hon'ble Court against Sr Edward Tir- whitt, Dame Ann Baildon, Christopher Colbye and others, to the intent that the said severall Indentures and defeazances, and the Statute or Recognizance and booke of Accounpte in the said Bill mencioned might be brought saffe and uncan- celled into this Court, to which Bill the Defend'ts on Trini- tye Tearme 2 Charles , putt in their severall Answeres, And Sr Edward Tirwhitt well knowing, that before the said lease of 99 yeares by him made to yo'r Orator and Thomas Colbye as aforesaid, he had fraudulently and w'th a purpose to defeate the said Sr Francis Baildon and to frustrate the lease, made some former secrett Conveighance or estate unto one Richard Smith and Robert Smith upon

48

secrett trust and confidence and for noe vallewable or good
consideracion and notw'thstanding the secrett and fraudulent
estates doth continew the reputed Owner thereof and doth
conceale the said secrett estates, for unless the same should
be discouered and the parties be made parties in Court, yo'r
Orator should not have any benefitt of any Decree to be
made in this Hon'ble Court against the said Sr Edward Tirwhitt upon the said former suite, and yo'r Orator sithence
the said Bill exhibitted hath had casuall intelligence of the
secrett assurances made by Sr Edward, And whereas by the
Answers of the said Christopher Colbye and Dame Ann
Baildon his mother, matters were soe handled that y'or
Orator could not discover thereby what was become of the
said writings and euidences, which by his Bill he did allsoe
seeke to discover, The said Christopher Colbye hath inge-
niously confessed sithence the said Bill exhibitted and answers
put in thereunto that yo'r euidences, Books of Accounpts,
etc, are sithence the answere of the said Defend'ts come to
the hands Custodie and possession of the said Christopher
Colbye and are in his power to produce nevertheles he de-
taineth the same from yo'r orator (Prays for discovery of the
secret estates and also of the documents in Christopher
Colbye's possession)   Signed Jo : Davies.

"The Aunswer of Christopher Colbye esquier (Sworn 19
Feb. 1626–7). He admits that since his answer to the
plaintiff's former Bill the documents referred to have come
into his possession but he hath since delivered them over to
John Freshwater of London gentleman in whose hands
they now are so far as he knows. Prays that the Bill may
be dismissed. Signed Simon English."

An *inquisitio post mortem* was held on the death of every tenant *in capite*,—that is to say, of those who held their lands directly from the crown and not of a "mesne" lord,—in consequence of the rule of feudal tenure that the heir, before he could take possession of his ancestors' lands, must pay a "relief" and homage to the king. These inquisitions were taken by an officer in each county, called the "escheator," whence the inquisitions themselves are sometimes, though erroneously, known as "escheats," in pursuance of writs, of which the most usual form was that *de diem clausit extremum*, directing him to hold an inquiry before a jury sworn to return a verdict on the following points :

1. What land the tenant died seised of.

2. The services by which the lands were held and their yearly value.

3. The date of the tenant's death.

4. The name and age of the heir.

The inquisition, after being engrossed on parchment, was returned into the King's Chancery, and a transcript sent to the Exchequer and Court of Wards and Liveries when the heir was an infant.

Inquisitiones Post Mortem.

Temp. Henry VIII. to Charles I. Part of the collection of the late Sir Charles Young, Garter King of Arms, in the library of the Herald's College, and were evidently compiled from Cole's Escheats in the British Museum.

Royal Denison Belden

Inquisitiones Post Mortem in Court of Wards.

FRANCISCUS BAYLDON WILES

This inquisition is of course in Latin, but as part of the skin was torn off and another part a good deal decayed, I have freely translated it.— *W. Paley Baildon.*

"Inquest held at Pontefract in the Co. of York 20th day of March in the year of the reign of James now King of England, France and Ireland the 21st & of Scotland the 57th before John Richardson Esquire the Escheator of our lord the King for the aforesaid Co. the King commanding the said Escheator & directing him by this Inquest annexed to inquire after the death of Francis Baildon late of Kipax in the Co. of York aforesaid Knight deceased on the oath &c. *Who say* on their oath aforesaid that the aforesaid Francis Baildon Knight in the said letter named the day before his death was seized in his demesne as of feeof & in one capital messuage or tenement in Kipax af's'd w'th the appurts called Kipax Hall w'th all bldgs and outbldgs and all lands meadows pasture and pasture lands woods underwoods rents & hereditaments whatso'r in Kipax aforesaid w'th the same messe or its appurt's usually held   And Also of and in all those yearly tithes from time to time arising coming and renewing in the   of Kipax   af's'd   And also of and in all those tithes of woll and lambs yearly & from time to time arising coming and renewing in or within the parish of Kipax   af's'd   And Also of and in all those tithes of grain & corn w'th the appurt's yearly and from time to time coming arising and renewing in Kipax

af's'd. *And also* of and in one storeh'se for tithes An-
glick 'a tyth barne' and one croft or p'cell of land adjoin'g
the same situate lying & being w'thout the walls or precints
of the vicarage of Kipax afores'd. *And also* of & in 4 acres
of meadow lying & being in the west meadow of Snaith &
Cowick in the Co. af's'd in a certain place there called 'le
yeoles' *And* also the Advowson donation & free disposition
of the parish church of Leethley in the af's'd County *And*
of and in all that messuage tenemt with all the lands meadows pasture & pasture land to the same appertaining or with
the same usually held late in the tenure or occupation of Gilbert Greenwood and Elizabeth Smyth or their assigns lying
& being in Ayrengden or Ayrinzden in the aforesaid County
And of and in a messe with all bldgs and outbldgs being in
the town of Byrom with a close of meadow called 'le moore
close' contain'g by estimation 4 acres of land wh'er more or
less in Byrom afores'd in the County afores'd *And* of and in
all that windmill with its appurts situate lying and being on
Staynforth in the Co. of York aforesaid of the lordship of
Hatfield in the Co. of York afores'd. And of & in a reversion after the death of Jane Metham late the wife of Alexander Metham* deceased in certain messes lands tenements
& other herd'ts lying and being on Cateby Sprodebrough
and Wilthropp in the Co. af's'd. *And* the af's'd Francis
Baildon senior of the messe lands tenem's & o'r prems' &c
(. . . . . MSS. undecipherable) by virtue of a lease was

---

* Alexander Metham of Cadeby eld. son of James by Joane dau of
   Cartwright als, vicar's, living 1585 m. Katherine da. of Andrew
Kellam of Hickleton.

WILLIAM BAILDON, OF BAILDON

Born 1562. (See page 25)

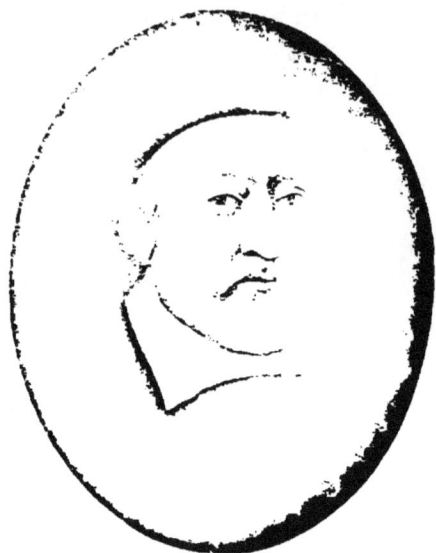

seized made in the name of Francis Baildon of Kipax senior
gentleman 22nd day of June in the 37th year of the reign
of Queen Elizabeth made sealed and delivered in writing of
which Inture or writing the tenor follows on these following words. 'To all faithful Christians to whom this present
written Indre' shall come Francis Bayldon senior of Kipax
in the Co. of York gentleman greeting in the Lord for ever
Know Ye that I the afores'd Francis Baildon for divers good
& sufficient reasons & consideration moving me thereto and
chiefly in fulfilling certain articles and agreement of marriage
specified in an Indenture made between Francis Haldenby
the Elder of Haldenby in the Co. of York esquire of the one
part and the afores'd Francis Baildon the Elder of the other
part through & in couson of a marriage had & solemnized
between Francis Baildon the younger son and heir of Francis Baildon the Elder & Elizabeth Haldenby daughter of
Robert Haldenby who was son and heir of the aforesaid
Francis Haldenby the Elder And also in full complement
pertain'g to a certain contract & agreement declared and set
out in a certain Ind're of Feoffment between one the afore'd
Francis Baildon of the one part and Hillary Baildon of
Snaith in the Co. of York gentleman and Anthony Haldenby of Crowle in the Co. of Lincoln gentleman the Feoffes
of the other part I have feoffed granted and by this present
writ'g confirmed to the afores'd Hillary Baildon and Anthony Haldenby their heirs and assigns one capital messe or
tenem't in Kipax af's'd called 'Kipax Hall' with all build'gs
& outbuildg's and w'th all other & any messuages or Cottages
in Kipax And all other & any tofts crofts barns stables
dovecotes orchards gardens closes meadows pastures lands

arrable woods underwoods rents reversions liberties ease-
ments profits emolum'ts & heredits whatsoever with their
appurts lying and being in the town fields territory & parish
of Kipax or with the same used occupied enjoyed or known
reputed or accepted to be as part parcell or member of the
premises one tithe called 'Clementety the' in Kipax only
excepted and reserved *To have and to hold* the aforesaid Capital messe or tenement called 'Kipax Hall' with all & singular other Ye messes cotles tofts crofts lands tenem'ts &
heredits whatsoever & all other the premises above ment'd
w'th the appts. except as af's'd *To* the af's'd Hillary Baildon & Anthony Haldenby & their heirs for ever *To* the
sole &pp benefit use and intent'n in this present
hereinaft set out & declared & to no oth benefits uses or intent'ns *To wit To have* one half or moiety of the af's'd capital messe or tenem't called 'Kipax Hall' & one half or
moiety of all & singul' oth' the messe lofts crofts build'gs
gardens orchards barns dovecotes closes meadows pastures
arrable land woods underwoods rents reversions lib'ties ease-
m'ts p'fits emolum'ts & heredits whats'r w'th their appurts
lying and being in the town fields territory & p'ish of Kipax
af's'd except as af's'd *To the* use & benefit of ye afores'd
Francis Baildon the elder & Margaret his wife during
Ye lives & for the life of the surv'or of them without any
impeachm't of waste And after the decease of the af's'd
Francis & Margaret then all & singul'r the p'mises w'th ye
app'ts to the use and benefit of the af's'd Francis Baildon
son and heir of the af's'd Francis Baildon ye elder and
Eliz'th his wife & the hrs male of ye body of the af's'd
Francis Baildon the younger of the body of ye af's'd Eliza-

Pedigree of Baildon of Kippax County-Yorks

beth betw'n them legitimately begotten or to be begotten &
for default of such issue Rem'r to ye hrs male of ye af's'd
Francis ye younger of his body legitimately begotten or after
this to be begotten   And for default of such issue then all
and singular ye prem's last set out wholly to remain to ye
hrs. male of ye body of ye af's'd Francis the elder legitimately begotten or after this to be begotten   And for default
of such issue then all and sing'r the p'mises last above set out
wholly to remain to the right hrs of the same Francis for
ever   And to Have and to Hold the other half or moiety of
the af's'd Capital messe or tenem't called 'Kipax Hall' &
the other moiety of all & singular Ye pr'mises above specified
w'th the appurts except as af's'd *To Ye* af's'd Hillary &
Anthony & th'r h'rs to the use & benefit of ye af's'd Francis
Baildon Ye elder & Margaret his wife during their natural
lives & for the life of the survivor of them w'thout any
impeachment of waste   And after the decease of the af's'd
Francis & Margaret all & singular the premises above specified To remain to the use & behoof of Ye af's'd Francis
Baildon Ye younger & the hrs male of his body rightly begotten or to be begotten   And for default of such issue then
all and singul' the prem's above set out To remain to the
heirs male of the af's'd Francis Bayldon the elder rightly
begotten or to be begotten   And for default of such issue
then all and singul' the prem's last set out wholly to remain
to the right heirs of the same Francis the elder for ever To
hold of the capital lord of the fee by the services therefor'
due & of right accustomed   In witness whereof I have to
this present Charter set my Seal the 22nd day of June the
37th year of Ye reign of our lady queen Elizabeth by the

grace of God Queen of England France & Ireland Defend
of the Faith &c. And that afterwards poss'on & seizin of
the messe & other p'mises in the afores'd wr't'g contain'd
was in the p'pr was delivered by the afores'd Francis Baildon
knt in the said litters named to the aforesaid Feoffees in the
said written Indenture named accord'g to the form of Ye said
written Indenture & its indorsem't The Jurors af's'd on the
taking of this inquest showing more fully as regards the
matter by virtue of a certain written Indre & by force of a
cert'n act of the Parliam't of our lord Henry the eighth late
King of England holden at Westminst' the 4th day of February in the y'r of his reign Ye 27th entitled for transfer'g
uses into possess'n ye af's'd Francis Bayldon Knt & ye af's'd
Margaret then his wife were seized of & in all and singul' ye
p'mises in the af's'd written Indre last ment'd in ye demesne
as of freehold for ye term of ye lives with remaind'r of one
half to the af's'd Francis Bailton (*sic*) ye younger & Elizabeth then his wife and the heirs male of the body of ye af's'd
Elizabeth begotten with reversion expectant thereon to the
right heirs of ye af's'd Francis Bayldon Knt for ever *Remainder* as to the other half expectant th'ron to ye af's'd
Francis Baildon ye younger & ye heirs male of his body
Revers'n expect't th'ron to ye right heirs of af's'd Francis
Baildon Knt for ever And the Jurors af's'd lastly say on
ye oath that because afterwards to wit ye 1st May 40 yr of
reign of Queen Elizabeth af's'd ye af's'd Margaret wife of
af's'd Francis Bayldon Knt died at Kipax af's'd & that
afterwards to wit 11 March A. D. 1712 (*sic*) af's'd Francis
Baildon ye younger died at Kipax af's'd seised of such estates in rem'r to his heir by the af's'd Elizabeth his wife

HALDENBY of Haldenby

ARMS VERT, A FESS BETWEEN 3 COVERED CUPS OR.

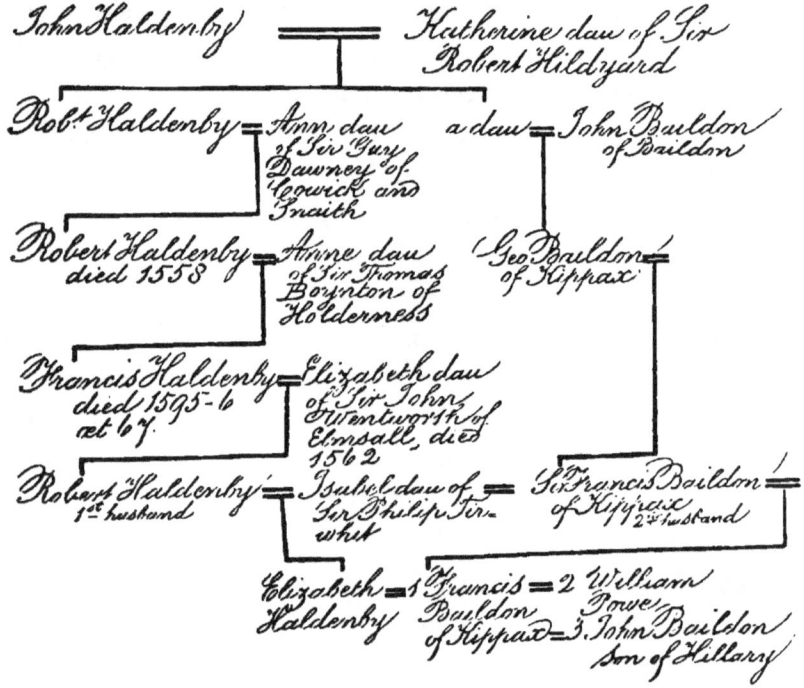

John Haldenby ═══ Katherine dau of Sir Robert Hildyard

Robt Haldenby ═ Ann dau of Sir Guy Dawney of Cowick and Snaith

a dau ═ John Baildon of Baildon

Robert Haldenby died 1558 ═ Anne dau of Sir Thomas Boynton of Holderness

Geo Baildon of Kippax

Francis Haldenby died 1595-6 æt 67 ═ Elizabeth dau of Sir John Wentworth of Elmsall, died 1562

Robert Haldenby 1st husband ═ Isabel dau of Sir Philip Tirwhit ═ Sir Francis Baildon of Kippax 2nd husband

Elizabeth Haldenby ═ 1 Francis Baildon of Kippax ═ 2 William Powe ═ 3 John Baildon son of Hillary

a certain Francis Bayldon gentleman. And that afterwards to wit on the 2nd day of May in ye 2nd year of ye reign of our said lord James now King of England France & Ireland the said Francis Baildon Knt took to wife one Anne Colby at Kipax af's'd And the afores'd Jurors lastly say on ye oath as af's'd that ye af's'd Francis Baildon Knt so as af's'd seized of other prem'es not mentioned in ye said written Ind're and being of sound memory ye 5th day of Nov'r in ye year of ye reign of our lord King James ye 13th 1615 made and delivered his last Will & Testament in writing inter alia on these English words following 'In the name of God Amen the fifte daie of November in the yeare of the Reigne of our Sovereign lord James by the grace of God of England Scotland & Ireland Kinge defender of the faith &c. the thirteenth & of Scotland the nine & fortieth Anno dni One thousand six hundred & fifteene Item I give and bequeath unto Richard Baildon and Henry Baildon my sons & their heirs all that the tythes of corne and graine yearely reneuinge arisinge and fallinge to be dewe within the town or lott of Kipax aforesaid & w'thin the demeasnes thereof & all that the tythe of wooll & lambes yearely reneuringe & fallinge to be dewe w'thin the p'ishe of Kipax af's'd To have and to hold the said tythes of corne & grayne of wooll & lambes in Kipax the demeasnes and p'ise thereof as is severally before lymitted unto the said Richard Bayldon & Henry Bayldon (*sic*) & their heires & assignes unto the rentts & payments thereout due & payable *Provided alwaies* & my will nevertheles is that the said Richard Bayldon & Henry Bayldon nor either of them nor their assignes shall not ent nor int meddle with

the said tythes nor any p'te of them durringe the space &
tyme of five yeares nexte after my decease duringe w'ch tyme
my will is that my supervisors shall take and receive the
profitts thereof to be bestowed as hereafter in theis p'sentes
is appoynted   Item I give and bequeath to Thomas Baildon
my sonne & his heires the rev con after the decease of
Barwick of all theis my messuages cottages lands & tenements in Cadby in the County of Yorke   And alsoe all that
my mesuage or tenements w'th divers lands & tenements
thereto belonginge in Eringdon in the County aforesaid
called Eringdon Parke w'ch I purchased of Master Read-
head and for w'ch I have his bond for generall warranty &
one windmyll in Staynforth in the lott of Hatfield in the
County aforesaid in the tenure of Henry Packyn gent.   Together also w'th the rev con of fower acres of meadowes in
Snailbinge in the County of Yorke after the decease of the
above named Dame Anne my wife   And also the advowson
donacon & p'sentacon of and to the p'she Church of Leethe-
ley in the County of Yorke w'th all & singular their appur-
tenaunces p'fitts & comodities to them or any of them belonginge To have and to hold all & every the above menconed
p'mises in Cadeby Eringedon Stayneforth leethley & Snaith
aforesaid to the said Thomas Bayldon his heires & assignes
for ever   And whereas in these presentes I have referred
many things in this my will to the oversight rule and dis-
posall of my sup'visors in this my last will to be named I doe
hereby intreate name and appoynte Sir Thomas Dawney and
Sir Henry Goodricke Knights Richard Hutton Esqr Sirient
at lawe Thomas Wentworth and John Colby Esqrs & the
said Robte Hawton sup'visors of this my last will and Testa-

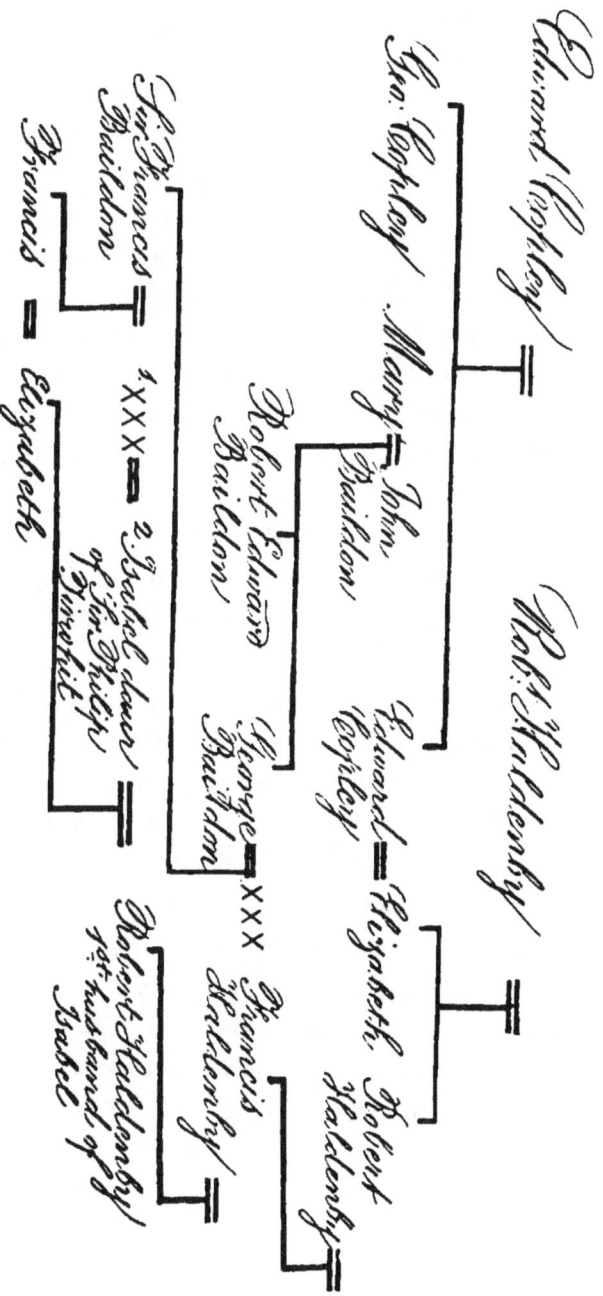

Edward Copley

Geo. Copley   Rob't Haldenby

Sir Francis   Mary = John   Edward = Elizabeth   Robert
Baildon   Baildon   Copley   Haldenby

Francis = Elizabeth   ¹ ××× ═ ² Isabel daur   Robert Edward   George ═ ×××   Francis
of Sir Philip   Baildon   Baildon   Haldenby
Fairhill

Robert Haldenby
1ˢᵗ husband of
Isabel

ment' And as to the af's'd will by evidence shown to the Jurors fully at the time of taking this inquest it appears *That* the af's'd Henry Baildon died in the lifetime of the s'd Francis Baildon the elder in the said letter named at London the 12th day of May A. D. 1618 And that the af's'd Thomas Baildon died in the lifetime of the af's'd Francis Baildon Knight at London the 20th day of November A. D. 1619 *And that* the af's'd Richard Bayldon is now surviving and living in full health at Kipax *And also* that the af's'd Francis Bayldon Knight died seized of the af's'd messuage & tenem't in Byrom af's'd in the af's'd written Indre in the af's'd will not mentioned *And* moreover ye Jurors say on their oath that the af's'd capital messe in Kipax called 'Kipax Hall' with all bldgs. lands tenem'ts & hereds. whats'r to the same app'tain'g as above mentioned was at the time of the death of the said Francis Baildon Knt held of the most excellent Prince Charles Prince of Wales in soccage as of his honor of Ponterfact p'cell of the Duchy of Lancaster by the rent of 4s. 1d. & ½d. yearly to be paid for the services to the af's'd honor from 3 weeks to 3 weeks and that it is of the clear yearly value exclusive of outgoings of 40s. And that all those yearly tithes from time to time arising in the land & demeasnes of Kipax af's'd at the time of ye death of ye af's'd Francis Bayldon Knt were held of the s'd most excellent prince Charles prince of Wales as of his af's'd honor of Pontefract by fealty as in free & common soccage & by a yearly rent of 20/s and 8d paid for all services and demands and are of the clear y'rly value exclusive of all outgoings of 20/s And that those other tithes of wool and lambs from time to time arising in Kipax af's'd at the time of ye death of ye s'd Francis Bayldon Knt were held of our said lord the King as of his manor of 'Eastgreenwich' in Co. Kent by fealty as in free and Common soccage and are of the clear yearly value exclusive of outgoings of 20/s And that all those tithes of grain y'rly arising in Kipax af's'd w'th a storehouse for tithes Anglice 'a tythe Barne' & a croft or p'cell of land lying adjacent af's'd at the time of the death of ye s'd Francis Bayldon Knt were held of our s'd lord the King & his heirs & successors as of his s'd manor of 'Eastgreenwich' in con Kent af's'd by fealty as in free & common soccage by the yearly rent of £7..6..8 for all services & demands & are of the clear yearly value exclusive of outgoings of 40/s And that ye said 4 acres of meadow in Snaith & Cowick af's'd in a certain place there called 'le yolles' were at the time of death of said Francis Baildon Knt held of s'd most excellent prince Charles prince of Wales as of his manor of Snayth in free & common soccage & is of clear yearly value after all outgoings of 6s/8d And that ye Advowson of the Parish Church of Leethley was at time of death of s'd Francis Baildon Knt held of ye King as of his s'd manor of 'Eastgreenw'ch' by fealty as in free soccage & is of no value because the church of Leethley is now filled by one Martin Fladden being the incumbent thereof And that ye messuage or ten'm't w'th appurts late in occupat'n of Gilbert Greenwood & Eliz'th Smyth or their assigns lying & being in s'd Ayringdon & ayringden P'ke in ye p'ish of Heptonstall in said Co. was at time of death of s'd Francis Baildon Knt held of King as of his lordship of Wakefield in free & common socage by fealty and is of clear yearly value after all outgoings of 3s/4d And that ye messee w'th appurts

in town of Byrom w'th a close of land called 'le moore close'
cont'g by estimat'n 4 A in Byrom of s'd was at time of
death of s'd Francis Bayldon Knt held of s'd prince as of
s'd honor of Pontefract by military service but to w'ch part
of military fee s'd Jurors not aware & is of clear y'rly value
after all outgoings of 6s/8d   And that af's'd wind mill w'th
appurts at Staynford at time of death of s'd Francis Baildon
Knt was held of King as of s'd manor of Eastgreenwich
by fealty in free & common soccage & by y'rly rent of 13s/4d
for all services & demands & is of clear y'rly value after all
outgoings of 6s/8d   *And* that the rev'sion of all y't messe
land and tenem't & other here's in Cadeby Sprodbrough &
Wilthropp was at time of death of s'd Francis Bayldon Knt
held of Godfrey Kopley Esq as of his manor of Sprotbrough
in free & common socage & is of clear y'rly value after all
outgoings of 20/s   And the Jurors lastly say on y'r oath the
said Sir Francis Baildon Knt died at Monck Friston in
af's'd County the 24th day of June y'r of James of England
20 and of Scotland 55 & that Francis Baildon son of af's'd
Francis Baildon ye younger deceased was & is consangin &
next heir of the af's'd Francis Baildon Knt deceased to wit
son & heir of af's'd Francis Baildon gentleman (son and
heir apparent of s'd Francis Baildon Knt) & Elizabeth wife
of s'd Francis Baildon gentleman & was aged at time of
death of s'd Francis Baildon Knt 16 year 4 months & 3
days   And that s'd Dame Anne Baildon late wife of s'd
Francis Baildon Knt is still living & in full health at Kipax
And that s'd Elizabeth late wife of s'd Francis Baildon gentleman is still living & in full health at Kipax & is now ye
wife of William Pow yeoman   And that s'd Jane Metham

late wife of Alexis Metham under the name of Jane Barwick
is still living & in full health at Doncaster. And lastly ye
Jurors say that s'd Richard Baildon one of ye younger sons
of s'd Francis Baildon Knt deceased immediately after ye
death of Sr Francis Baildon Knt took possession of the rents
& profits of all & singul' the tithes of grain & lands in ye
demeasne & town of Kipax af's'd from the time of death of
s'd Francis Baildon Knt up to day of taking this inquest And
that s'd William Pow took possession of messe in Kipax
call'd Kipax Hall with appurts from the time of death
of s'd Francis Baildon Knt up to the day of holding this inquest And that s'd Dame Anne Baildon took possession of
profits of tithes of wool and lambs in p'ish of Kipax af's'd &
of s'd 4 A of meadow in Snaith & Cowick & of s'd windmill
in Staynford from time of death of s'd Francis Baildon Knt
up to day of holding this inquest And that Gabriel Bur-
dett took profits of lands & tenem'ts in Ayringden & Ayringden p'h from time of death of s'd Francis Baildon Knt
deceased up to the day of holding yt inquest And that
John Burridge took profits of land & tenem'ts in Byrom
af's'd from time of death of s'd Francis Baildon Knt up to
day of holding ye inquest and lastly s'd Jurors say on ye
oath that s'd Francis Baildon Knt on the day that he died
did not have or hold any other or more lands tenem'ts or
hdts. in possession revcon rem'r or use of our s'd lord ye
King or of any other person whomsoever other than as aforesaid is set out as being shewn to them

"In witness &c."

Being not certain of my
sister Bridges ship at to inform you of [...]
I shall by the favor of you to inform me [...]
[...] my last [...] & to render my
[...] [...] to do [...] let me
know if she is [...] to [...] & how
she recovers [...] shall her visit me [...]
[...] [...] she look? [...] my sister
& sister be [...] [...] [...]
me to them for all my [...] [...]
that [...] respected think [...] my
remember me kindly to [...] [...] I beg
my [...] & [...] time [...]
I [...] my [...] you are [...]
I tender my services [...]

yors affectionately to
serve you [...]

Captain Baynes

July 6th /52

Royal Denison Belden

Chancery Proceedings, Miscellaneous, Series 1, *Part* 22, *No.* 43.

"10th June 1623

"Humblie shewe unto yo'r good Lo'pp yo'r daily Orators Richard Bayldon, Cuthbert Bayldon and Martyn Bayldon Gentlemen, Three of the younger sonnes of Sr Francis Bayldon, late of Methley, in the County of Yorke, Knight, deceased, Laurence Kighley, gentleman, and Clare his wife, and Edmond Chatterton gentleman, and Muriall his wife, twoe of the daughters of the said Sr Francis Bayldon, being all the children of the said Sr Francis by his second wife Margaret, That whereas the said Sr Francis Bayldon att the tyme of his death was seised in his demesne as of feeof divers Mannors, lands, Tenements and hereditamts Freehold and Coppihold, within the County of Yorke and, elsewhere, to the yearely value of £150, and was also possessed Chattells realls and personalls to the value of £3000 at the least. And made his last will and Testament in writing bearing date the 5th day of November in the 13th yeare of his Ma'tie's raigne and lived divers yeares after, And by the same will did devise to Dame Anne his then third wife all that one halfe parte of the Parke in Snayth and Cowick called Phippin Parke and the herbage and pawnage thereof for the terme of Three yeares and after for such severall Termes as he then had therein, if the said Dame Anne should so long live (etc mentioning other legacies) together with divers other legacies of good value, thereby declaring (as the truth was) that shee was to take the same legacies in satisfaccion of her whole Righte to all the goods and lands of the said Sr Francis Bayldon : And the said Sr Francis (having an in-

63

tenc'on that his whole Interest in the said Phippin Parke
should come unto yo' said Orators after the death of same
Anne, or immediatelie, if shee should refuse her legacie) did
by the same last will and testament will that his children
that should have Phippin Parke assigned to them should
yearely pay, after they have possession of his parte thereof to
his Neece Anne Mirfield, wife of George Mirfield the somme
of 53s. 4d. at o'r Ladie Day and the Feast of St Michaell
yearely by equall porcions so long as the terme of yeares to
them assigned should indure if the said Anne Mirfield should
so long live. And after divers other legacies and bequests
the said Testator did geve the rest of his goods Chattells and
Credits to yo'r said Orators and to Henry Bayldon and
Thomas Bayldon sithence, deceased, equallie to be devided
amongest them : And the said Sr Francis (being in his life
possessed of the said moiety of the said Parke called Phippin
Parke for certayne yeares yett enduring, being a parte and
residue of a terme of one and forty yeares in possession by
lease from the late Queene Elizabeth at a yearely rent, and
being allso possessed by lawfull meanes afterwards from one
Thomas Fanshawe Esq. in the graunt of the whole herbage
and pawnage of the said Parke in Revercion for one and
Twenty yeares by and under a lease thereof made by the
Kings most excellent Ma'tie that now is at a like yearely
rent) about the 16th yeare of His Ma'tie's raigne did assigne
all his interest and estate in the moiety of the Parke and
other the last mencioned premisses in possession and Revercion unto Sr Thomas Smyth, Knight, together w'th the severall Indentures of the Criginall graunts and leases thereof
and all the meane Conveyances and writings touching the

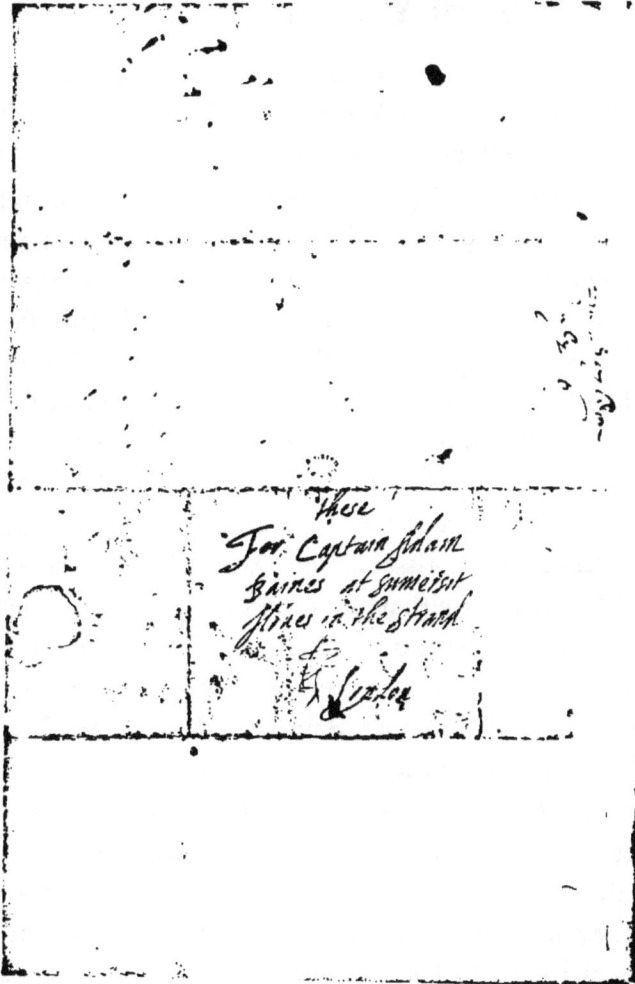

These

For Captain Adam
Baines at Somerset
stares in the strand

Lizlee

Back of Letter from James Baildon

same, upon this Condicion in the said Charter of assignment Conteyned, That if £400 were satisfied by the said Sr Francis, his executors or administrators, unto the said Sr Thomas Smyth at certayne dayes and places specified, then the assignemt should be voyde and that Sr Thomas Smyth should thereupon redeliver up all deeds and writings w'ch formerlie he had from Sr Francis: And w'th this further Agreem't also that if the said £400 were not payd, whereby the whole interest of the premisses should happen to become absolute and without condicion to Sr Thomas Smyth, That he would then satisfie Sir Francis his executors or administrators, so much more money about the said £400 as the estates of the said premisses should be worth Bona fide to be sold oughtright or else that upon receipt of such moneys, as should be justlie due unto him by the said Sr Francis or his assignes, he would reconvey the premisses (etc); w'ch Conveyance the said Sr Thomas Smyth doth acknowledge, But whether the said condicion were therein conteyned or noe yo'r said Orators cannott discover, but the said Sr Thomas Smyth doth now refuse to deale for the premisses outright or for any absolute enioying thereof to himself by geveing any more money for the same, though he hath bene thereunto required on the behalf of yo'r said Orators to whome the same is lymitted by the same will amongest the goods and chattells of the said Sr Francis not formerlie given and disposed of, For that the said Dame Anne Bayldon, to whome the moiety of the said Phippen Parke is by the said will mencioned to be geven, hath disclaymed and refused the legacies geven her by the will, and for her greater advantage and preferment hath betaken her to the thirds of her said husband's lands of

5

Inheritance, And for that the said Sr Francis had not power to dispose of his present Interest in the said premisses by his will, the same being Morgaged and forfeited to Sr Thomas in the life tyme of Sr Francis:

"Now so it is may it please yo'r good Lo'pp that Sr Francis Bayldon having named Sr Thomas Downey, Sr Richard Hutton, one of his Ma'tie's Justices of his court of Common Pleas, and divers other Gentlemen of worshipp and qualitie, to be the Executors of his said will, and leaving his estate much encombred, the said Executors refused to take upon them the burthen and trouble thereof, And the said Dame Anne Bayldon taking advantage thereof hath procured Letters of Administracion to be graunted unto her of the goods and chattells of the said Sr Francis (cum Testamento annexo) and by Coulo' thereof hath possessed herself of all his personall Estate, and to the entent to make a further benefitt unto herself by the redemcion of the said morgaged premisses, and so stripps yo'r poore Orators of all the benefitt that thereby by the lymittacion of the said will ought to redound unto them for their maintenance. The said Dame Anne · Bayldon in the vacacion tyme, That is to say, upon the last day of March now last past, in very secrette manner as administratrix did prefere a Bill of Complaint unto this hono'ble court against Sr Thomas Smyth, thereby setting forth that shee had lately offered unto him one that would deale w'th him for the premisses, and satisfie him for all moneys due unto him w'ch Course was concluded and agreed upon betwene them to have the countenance of the decree of this hono'ble Court to passe the premisses over to such person or persons as the said Dame should appoynt thereby, to leave yo'r Orators remedilesse, w'ch Course was prosecuted accordinglie, for that the answere of the said Sr Thomas was recorded in this hono'ble Court the first day of Aprill last past being the next day after the Bill was recorded whereby it appeareth that Sr Thomas, out of his worthy disposicion, is willing to accept his due dett w'th reasonable dammages and to assign the premisses as the Court shal be pleased to order : Inasmuch therefore as Dame Anne hath disclaymed any benefitt by the said will by accepting her Thirds, and therefore ought not now as Administratrix to have the benefitt of Redempcion, but the same ought to redound unto yo'r said Orators by the lymittacion of the said will as goods and chattells not devised yo'r Orators being otherwise very meanely provided for out of their Father's Estate. And for that they are ready and willing to pay unto Sr Thomas Smyth all such moneys as are justlie due unto him (etc). To the intent that upon payment thereof he may be ordered to Convey his Interest in the premises to yo'r Orators or to such person or persons as they shall appoynt, and that all Proceedings upon the Bill exhibited by Dame Anne may bee stayed and that she may be ordered forth w'th to pay so much of the profitts of the said Phippin Parke as shee hath received since the death of her said husband unto the said Sr Thomas, to th' end that yo'r Orators (whome the said Dame Anne hath diverslie wronged by delaying their dues from them and by stirring upp unjust sutes and vexacions against them) may thereby be somewhat eased in their paym't (Pray for writ of subpena to Sir Thomas Smyth and Dame Anne Bayldon to appear and answer)."

Beldens Coat of Arms, Embroidered

Concerning One Branch of the Descendants of Richard Bayldon

Richard
Baptized May 26, 1591; died 1655

Samuel
Born 1629; died 1713

Stephen
Born 1658; died 1720

Stephen
Born 1689; died 1736

Moses
Born 1726; died 1826

Augustus
Born 1753; died 1831

Royal Denison
Born 1795; died 1868

Augustus Cadwell
Born 1820; died 1896

Children:

Alvin Jackson
Born 1848

James Mead
Born 1852

Charles Gilbert
Born 1857

James Jerome
Born 1825

Child:

Harriet
Born 1858
Died 1860

Mead
Born 1833; died 1876

Children:

Edward Mead
Born 1865

Anna Louise
Born 1867

Edith
Born 1869

Olive Gertrude
Born 1873

RICHARD BAYLDON

TO record the history of the descendants of any man who came to America between the years 1607 and 1657 is to individualize the history of the country. The men who landed on these shores during those fifty years were actuated by the same purpose, filled with the same determination, and realized fully their dangers by sea and land.

A man of the present generation who looks back over the two hundred years and more is filled with justifiable pride if he finds a prototype in some ancestor from whom he has inherited the attributes which have made him successful.

A brief reference to the condition of England seems necessary to show the reason of such a large emigration during the years 1635–36. From March, 1629, to April, 1640, the Houses of Parliament were not convoked, and during this part of the reign of Charles I. the provisions of the Petition of Right were violated systematically; a large part of the revenue was raised without legal authority, and persons obnoxious to the government were cast into prison.

Lord Wentworth, Earl of Strafford, courageous, clever, and cruel, was the military and political counsellor. What Richelieu was to France he aspired to be to England. His policy was to put the estates and personal liberty of the people at the disposal of the crown, and to punish all who applied for relief or differed from the acts of the government.

William Laud was the Archbishop of Canterbury. He was a narrow, superstitious fanatic, and the nearest to Rome and the least in sympathy with the Reformation of all the archbishops of England. The people were so afraid of him that they concealed their hatred of the Church and pretended to conform. He had a complete system of spies, so that even private devotions were often interfered with.

Through the Star Chamber and the High Court the government could fine, imprison, pillory, and mutilate without restraint. The northern counties were under the surveillance of the Council of York, of which Lord Wentworth was president. "The tyranny of this council had made the Great Charter a dead letter." The people were in despair, and the dangers of the deep and uncertainty of the new country were preferable to such civil and spiritual despotism. Numerous colonies were already established in New England, and the government of England looked upon them with fear and aversion, but could not prevent their being augmented by constant emigration.

From a Letter written by William Paley Baildon, F.S.A., Member of the Council of the Archæological Society of Yorkshire.

"There is only one family of Bayldon; all persons bearing that name by inheritance must have sprung from the Yorkshire manor of that name. Richard Bayldon, son of Sir Francis Bayldon, of Kippax, baptized May 26, 1591, was the only Richard, so far as I know, who would have had money to spend in the purchase of land, as Richard of Wethersfield did.

"Richard Bayldon, of Wethersfield, was a man of some substance; whatever his motives for emigrating may have been, he was clearly in a very different position from so many of the early settlers, who had nothing beyond their clothes and a few cooking utensils. His whole career shows him also to have been a man of mark, a 'man of affairs,' one to whom his fellow-townsmen looked up; he was also presumably a man of education, and, judging from the actions of his descendants, he was also a man of fighting instincts. All these are Kippax characteristics.

"The coat of arms in the possession of the descendants of Richard is identical with the one used by the Bayldons of Bayldon and Kippax."

1613. "XXVI o Martin, 1613

"Richard Bayldon, aged 19 yeres, borne at Kippax in Com. Ebor, intending to pass over for Bredaugh to be a souldier under Capen Blundell,* hath taken the oath of allegiance.

Among the original settlers of Wethersfield, Connecticut, was Richard Bayldon, who came from Yorkshire, England, in the year 1635.

The settlers of Wethersfield were Puritans or Nonconformists, not Pilgrims, called Separatists or Brownists.

* Afterwards Sir George Blundell.

73

Ancestors and Descendants of

On the first emigrant land records of Wethersfield is the following:

"The 2d month & 7th daie 1641.

"The Lands of Ric Bayldon (those given him by the towne and those he bought of Jonas Wod) lying in Wethersfield on Connecticut river one piece whereon his house standeth, con three (acr) one rood more or less. The ends abut against Broad Street north and the lands of Ma Mitchell south; the sides against the way leading into ye plain west and the house-lot of Leysley Broadfield east. One piece lying in the Great Mead, con three acres more or less. The ends abut against the highway west, & the mea of the Wid Mason east; the sides against the mea of Sam Sherman south, and the aforesaid Wid Mason north. One other piece also lying in the Great Mead, con two acr more or less. The ends abut against the highway north, & the mead of Wid Mason south; the saides against the mead of Ro Parcke east, & Mr. Evans west. One other piece also lying in the Great Mea, con two acr more or less. The ends abut against the highway east & Back lots west; the sides against the mead of Tho Curtice north & lately Ed Wods & now Gorg Willis Esquire lies south. One piece lying in the Back lots being six (?) acr mead and swamp more or less. The ends abut against the way in the Wes swamp west, & the mead fence east, the sides against the lands of Ric Wastcoat north, and lands of Thurston Rayner, Andr Ward & Wid. Brundish south. One piece lying in the south field upland and swamp, con eighteen acr (mea & swamp erased) & one half more or less. The ends abut against the highway leading towards Maltabezick west, and the plain east; the sides against

74

the lands of Nat. Dickinson south & Jo Fletcher north. One piece also in the South Field, con thirteen acr, one half more or less. The ends abut against the aforesaid way leading to Maltabezicke east and lands not laid out west, the sides against the lands of Leysley Broadfield's south, & Na Dickinson north.

"One piece lying in the Dry Swamp in the east side of East Fields, con ten acr, more or less. The ends abut against a way leading out of the Great mead into mile mead east, and the middle line west; the sides against the lands of Ja Waterhouse south, and Tho Wright north."

October, 1654, he gave his son Samuel a piece of land. In the Colonial records of Connecticut are the following references to Richard Bayldon. 1643. "Richard Belding is bownd in £XX., George Chappell in £10 that the sd. George keepe good behawior and appeare the next Court. June the 5th, 1646, Rich Belding stands bownd in £20. Robt. Rugge in £40, that Rugge keepe good behawior and appeare the next Court. 24th April 1649. Peter Blatchford made oath in Courte that at the latt'r end of the last yeare, he delivered aboard of Chichester's vessell to Mr. Blackleach, by ye order of Jarius Mudge for the acco't of Rich. Belden six bush. of wheat and three of peas."

During the summer of 1650, Richard Belden received a grant of land in New London.

Richard Belden married in England and had two sons,— Samuel and John.

The following inventory of his personal property was found in the first volume of Wethersfield records in the office of the Secretary of State of Connecticut. The spelling of the name was changed between 1641 and 1643, and at the

present day different branches of the family use Baildon,
Belden, Belding, and Beldin.

"The Inventory of ye goods and cattles of & belonging to
ye estate of Richard Beldin of Wethersfield deceased taken
ye 22 of August, 1655.

	£	s	d
Impri, In ye parlor, one feather bed 1 pair of sheets, 2 blanketts, one coverlet and rugs, two pillows with ye bed-stead	06	00	00
It, one bed case, one boulster, one pair of sheets, one blankett, one cotton rugg, one pillow beere	04	00	00
It, one pair of flaxen sheets, two pillow beeres	01	10	00
It, one Diepr Table cloath, 13 napkins	01	05	00
" 10 pieces of pewter	01	06	00
" in two quart potts, one candle stick, 5 ockemey spoons, one silver spoone, other small things	01	10	00
It, one cubbard, one table forme to chest and other small things	02	15	00
It, In his wearing cloathes	06	00	00
" one musket, one karbine, one Rapier	03	00	00
" in ye kitchen, foure brass kettles, other small brass	04	00	00
It, two Iron potts, 4 cob irons, tramles and other iron ware	04	00	00
It, one table c forme, 3 chayers, one skrene, 3 cushings	01	06	00
It. In wooden ware and earthen vessells, tinn ware, with one smoothing iron	03	10	00
It. In working tools with one Gridstone	07	00	00
It. In ye chamber, in bedding and hogsheads with some other things	03	00	00
It. In Timber for wheeles and boultes for S'thing else	03	00	00
It. In two cows	11	10	00
" " swine	04	00	00
In 15 acres of corne and seaven akers of grass being gathered into ye barne	40	00	00
In 5 skeps of beefe	02	10	00
In a winnowing sheete and forks	00	15	00
In two hows, 4 baggs	01	00	00
	11	19	00

JOHN TALLCOTT.
JOHN NOTT.

Concerning Samuel Belding, the Hatfield Massacre, and the Falls Fight

Richard
1591–1665

Samuel
1629–1713

1675

THE treaty made by Governor Carver and Massasoit in 1620 was kept inviolate for more than fifty years.

Massasoit died in 1660, and four years before his death he took two of his sons to Plymouth and asked that they be given English names. The oldest son was called Alexander, the other Philip.

In 1661, Alexander was suspected of hostile designs and was taken to Plymouth. On the way he died, his enemies said of fever, but it was believed by his squaw, Weetamoo, that the English poisoned him. This wrong was not forgotten when, fourteen years later, she joined Philip and added to his warriors three hundred of her own. In 1671 some Indians murdered a white man in Dedham, and Philip was suspected of having instigated the crime. Boston called upon Philip for an explanation, and demanded that all English arms in the possession of his tribe should be delivered in Boston. This was considered an aggression by the Indians, and many acts of the English were looked upon with suspicion. In 1675 a friendly Indian was murdered for having warned the English of the hostile feeling of the tribes, and upon the testimony of one Indian three were caught, tried by a jury of six Englishmen and six Indians, and put to death. This seemed to be the last straw, and on June 24, 1675, the people of Swansea were attacked. This was the beginning of what is known as King Philip's War.

In May, 1676, news came that Indians were planting the deserted acres of Deerfield. Many of them were in camp about the Falls, which were afterwards named for Captain Turner.

When the message came, Captain Turner, who was in command of the valley forces, gathered a hundred mounted men at Hatfield for a night ride through Deerfield and Whately. The Indians heard the hoof-beats, but, as Captain Turner avoided the ford, they thought a herd of moose had crossed the river. At daybreak of May 10 they came upon the main encampment. Leaving their horses in the ravine, the company, by a slight detour, came upon the rear of the Indians. The surprise was so complete that over three hundred Indians were killed. But suddenly there came a rumor that Philip was near with a thousand braves. A panic seized the troops, and many were killed. Captain Turner fell, and Captain Holyoke took command. He reached Hatfield with the remainder of the band, but died soon after from the fatigue and excitement.

This war lasted over a year, and came to an erd soon after the death of Philip. Thirteen towns were destroyed, six hundred buildings burned, six hundred men killed, and many wounded.

SAMUEL BELDING

Samuel Belding, a survivor of the Falls fight, was the son of Richard Belden, and born in England. He was in Wethersfield with his father, and between the years 1644

Site of Samuel Bebings House in Kingston Massachusetts

and 1660 was in Totoket, now Brandford. In 1661 he was
in Hatfield, and fought in King Philip's War, the last rally
of Paganism against Christianity. His first wife, Mary, was
killed by the Indians, September 19, 1677. A party of
twenty-six Indians under command of Ashpelon descended
the Connecticut Valley and fell upon the town. It was
about ten o'clock in the morning; the men were busy in the
meadows or building a house outside the palisades. Three
men were shot down; then proceeding to the houses, nine
persons were killed, four wounded, seventeen taken captive,
and seven buildings burned. Alice Baker, of Cambridge,
read the following description of the massacres at Hatfield
and Deerfield at the field meeting of the Pocumtuck Valley
Memorial Association, held at Deerfield in 1872:

"It was the morning of the 19th of September, 1677.
A year had passed since the close of the war, and the
people of this valley, relieved of their apprehensions, were
beginning to resume their usual occupations, when the shrill
war-whoop rang through the frosty air, and a party of Indians, descending with fire and slaughter upon Hatfield,
ran hence with seventeen captives, mostly women and children, towards Deerfield. It was near sunset of one of those
tranquil autumn days we all know so well. Nought of
melancholy was in the song piped by a belated August
cricket, and the striped snake crawled from his hole to bask
in the sunshine as if he half believed summer had come
again. The witch-hazel threw into the lap of October a
wealth of blossoms which June could never extort from her.
A crown of gold, gemmed with opal and amethyst, rested
on the brow of the western hills, the swamps were ablaze

6

with the flame-colored sumachs. The mountain, already in shadow, seemed like some massive temple, where in stoles of scarlet, purple, and gold stood maple and oak and chestnut, like cardinal, bishop, and priest, to offer a sacrament of peace. No sound in the woodlands save now and then as a leaf nestled down softly and was silent, and the squirrels, as they frolicked among the branches, ceased their chatter, startled by the echo of Quentin Stockwell's hammer as it was borne up from the valley. Near by him were John Root and the child Samuel Russell, when suddenly, with great shouting and shooting, the Indians came upon them. Dropping their tools and seizing their guns, the men fled towards the swamp, where Root was instantly killed and Stockwell was overpowered and made captive. The prisoners were bound, and, as the night deepened, were led over the mountain 'in dark and hideous wayes,' the Indians as they travelled making 'strange noises of Wolves and Owles and other Wild Beasts, to the end that they might not lose one another; and if followed they might not be discovered by the English.' Among the Hatfield captives was Sarah Coleman, a little child. Her mother was slain, but the little girl endured the hardships of the long march, and when she was ransomed, eight months later, one little shoe, tattered and torn, was clinging to her foot. That shoe was given to her by her father the day she married, and has been handed down from generation to generation until more than two hundred years have passed, and now it is preserved among the relics of the Pocumtuck Valley Memorial Association."

Samuel Belding had seven children by his first wife. He

married (secondly) Mary, widow of Thomas Wells; (thirdly) Mary, widow of John Allis, and (fourthly) widow of John Wells.

An old record in the state papers of the Colony of Massachusetts Bay reads in this wise: "In answer to petition of Jonathan Wells, son to Mary Belding, his mother, petitioning in his behalf being a wounded man and by his wounds lost two yeares and the Court it judgeth it meet to referr the petition for relief to the Committee for wounded men.

"LYMAN BRADSTREET,

"*Gov.*

"15–Oct. 1680."

From the Colonial Records of Connecticut:
"General Court of Election.
21st of May 1657.

JOHN WINTHROP, *Gov.*

THOMAS WELLS, ESQ., *Deputy.*

Made free—Samuel Belding."

Samuel Belding was first in Hatfield about 1661. His house lot was on the east side of the present Main Street and very near the centre. His estate at that time was valued at one hundred pounds.

In the distribution of land to the proprietors, each one hundred pounds drew twenty-seven acres of tillage land in the several meadows and plains. All the rest of the land, with the exception of house lots, was held in common for a number of years and then divided.

Royal Denison Belden

Samuel Belding was prominent in church and town affairs, was often on committee to procure ministers. He was also selectman. Many of his descendants are now living in Hatfield and Whately. He died January 3, 1713.

Concerning Stephen Belding the Elder, a Survivor of the Falls Fight

Richard
1591–1655

Samuel
1629–1713

Stephen
1658–1720

STEPHEN BELDING

SAMUEL, the eldest son of Samuel Belding, married, in 1678, Sarah Billings, and it was a foregone conclusion that when the father married for his second wife the widow Wells, Stephen, the second son, would fall in love with her charming daughter, Mary. Stephen was just twenty and Mary fourteen, but responsibility came early to pioneer people, and there was time for wooing even during the Indian wars. We can easily imagine the dreadful anxiety of the young girl when Stephen was off on scouts, and is it not possible that when he came home from some dangerous mission that then was the time she gave the final "yes"? Life was too earnest for coquetry, and the August after Stephen was twenty-four and Mary eighteen they were married. They had nine children. Stephen died October 6, 1720, in his sixty-second year, and his widow married Captain Joseph Field, of Sunderland, and died March 15, 1751.

Massachusetts Archives, vol. lxix. p. 27.

"Steven Belden aged about 17 years testifyath yt he riding behind a Jonathan Wells saw Isacka Harrison on ye ground riding up, and heard call to ye man yt was on his horse three or 4 Rods before to take him up saying he could ride now; the man would not but rode away; then he spake to Jonathan wells to call backe ye man; both Jonathan and I called him back but he would not go back; and further saith not. This was as they were returning from ye right at ye falls."

Endorsed, "Severall evidences from Hadley as to Harrison's Death & etc. Belcher: returned 1st July 1676."

Many years after, in 1735, Samuel Hunt petitioned "Ye Court" for a grant of land to the survivors of the Falls fight. In 1736 a grant of six miles square was made. It was located on the north bounds of Deerfield and called Falls Fight Town, finally Bernardston.

STEPHEN BELDING'S WILL

"In the name of God, Amen, The twenty-third day of Septemb. in the Seventh year of ye Reign of our Sovereign Lord George by ye Grace of God of Great Brittain, France & Ireland King Defendr. of ye faith, &c., Annoqr. Domini 1720. I, Stephen Belding of Hatfield in ye County of Hampshire in his Majest's Province of ye Massachusetts Bay in New England, Husbandman, beeing very sick and week of body but of perfect mind and memory, Thanks be given unto God, Therefore calling unto mind the mortality of my body and knowing yt it is appointed to all men once to die, do make and ordain this my last will and testament, That is to say principally and first of all I give and recommend my Soul into the hands of God that gave it and my body I recommend to ye earth to be buried in decent Christian Burial at ye discretion of my executors hereinafter named nothing doubting but at ye Gen'l Ressurection I shall receive ye same again by ye Mighty power of God, and as touching such worldly Estate wherewith it has pleased God to Bless me in this life, I give devise and dispose of the same in the following manner and form.

"IMPRIS—My will is ye my just debts due to any and all persons whomsoever be first discharged to-gether with my funeral charges out of my estate by my executors hereinafter named.

"ITM. I give and bequeath to my loving wife Mary one third part of my personal or moveable estate during ye term of her natural life for her subsistance improvement and convenient well being and ye use of one half of my home lot house barn and orchard standing therein in Hatfield aforesaid. Alsoe do order will and bequeath her ye sum of Ten pounds yearly as an yearly revenue and income for subsistance during ye term of her natural life to be paid to her by my four sons Stephen Belding, Sam'l Belding, Jonathan Belding and Joshua Belding equally fifty Shillings each, yearly during ye term of her natural life.

"ITM. I will and bequeath to my oldest son Stephen Belding what I have already advanced on him amounting (as I judge) near to an Hundred pounds as alsoe an equal part of my real and personal estate with ye rest of my three sons above mentioned.

"ITM. I will and bequeath to my son Sam'l Belding an equall part or share of all my real and personal estate with ye rest of my three sons above named as alsoe with what I have advanced on him already out of my estate so much as will make him equal with my son Jonathan Belding, his being computed at forty-five pounds as money.

"ITM. I give and bequeath to my son Jonathan Belding what I have already advanced on him out of my estate which

I judge and compute to be fourty-five pounds as money as alsoe an equal part of my real and personal estate with ye rest of my three sons aforesaid.

"ITM. I give and bequeath to my son Joshua Belding an equal part of my real and personal estate with ye rest of my three sons aforesaid. As alsoe thirty pounds more to be advanced on him out of my estate more then to make him equal with his brethren Sam'l, and Jonathan which will be in the whole Seventy-five pounds, Joshua having as yet nothing advanced on him.

"ITM. I give and bequeath to my daughter Elizabeth Scot, alias Belding (besides what has been advanced on her already) ye sum of twenty pounds, in or as money.

"ITM. I give and bequeath to my daughter Mary Waite alias Belding (besides what I have advanced on her already) ye sum of twenty pounds in or as money.

"ITM. I give and bequeath to my youngest daughter Esther Belding ye sum of Fifty pounds in or as money.

"ITM. My will is yt what of my real estate falls by this my will to any of my sons afores'd and either or any of them be disposed to make sale thereof they shall make tender of it to some of their brethren allowing them a reasonable time for payment therefor if they be inclined to purchase ye same.

"ITM. My will is that my executors hereinafter named have ye term of eight years after my decease for ye payment of legacies afores'd, to my daughters.

"ITM. My will is that the estate willed my loving wife Mary after her decease be and descend to my four sons afores'd to be equally divided between them.

"ITM. My will is that my son Jonathan Belding pay to my executors the ten pound money which I lent him and he was to pay me it again.

"FINALLY. I will make constitute and appoint my loving wife Mary Belding and my son Sam'l Belding Executors of this my last will and testament and I do hereby utterly disallow revoke and disannull all and every other and former testaments, wills legacies and bequests and executors by me in any ways before named willed and bequeathed, rattifying and confirming this and no other to be my last will and testament

"In witness whereof I have hereunto set my hand and seal the day and year first above written.

Stephen Belding (Seal.)

"Signed, sealed, published, pronounced and declared by ye said Stephen Belding as his last will and testament in the presence of us ye subscribers hereunto. Thomas Hastings, Scribe, John Belding, Sam'll Gillett, John Hastings.

"Thomas Hastings, John Belding, Sam'll Gillett and John Hastings personally appeared in Hatfield this 29th day of October 1720.

"Before me under named, Judge of Probate and made Oath that they being present and did see Stephen Belding Sign and Seal this instrument in the sev'll pages of it as his last will and testament and yt he was of sound mind and memory when he did it and his wid'w Mary and his son

Royal Denison Belden

Sam'll who are nominated executors to this will and testament accepted of their executorship and thereupon,
  "I do approve and allow this will and testament.
      "Attest

                    "Sam'll Partridge
                      "*Judge of Probate.*"

Main Street, Northfield Massachusetts

Mill-Brook Northfield, Massachu

Concerning Stephen Belding the Younger, with a Few Anecdotes of his Brother Jonathan's Family

.

Richard
1591–1655

Samuel
1629–1713

Stephen
1658–1720

Stephen, Jr.
1689–1736

STEPHEN BELDING, JR.

THE English name Northfield was given to the northernmost settlement on the Connecticut River in 1672. It is bounded on the east by Warwick, on the south by Erving, on the southwest by Gill, on the west by Bernardston, on the north by the State line, which separates it from Vernon, Hinsdale, and Winchester. The Connecticut River divides the town into two unequal parts. The Ashuelot River also crosses Northfield, and the beautiful mill brook rushes through a gorge, and furnished the power for the first grist-mill built in 1685.

Stephen Belding, the eldest son of Stephen, was born February 22, 1689, in Northfield, Massachusetts. He married Mindwell, daughter of Captain Benjamin Wright, December 24, 1713, and died February 19, 1736.

Up to the year 1716 no forts had been built in Northfield, but the war which broke out in June alarmed the people, and in the course of the summer two were begun,—one on the Field lot and one on the Stephen Belding lot. Captain Benjamin Wright was the head of the militia.

"December 17th, 1716.

"Conditions of agreement betwixt Steven Belden of Swampfield and the inhabitants of Northfield with the consent of ye committee for Northfield are as followeth—The said Belden shall have 15 acres of land in Bennett's meadow and labour, as below said *provided* ye said Belden builds a

95

sufficient grist mill and maintain it forever; if said Belden neglect or fail to maintain or refuse said mill for the Town's use, then said mill with iron and stone and with all appurtenance thereto belonging to return to the town; and said mill to be going by next Michaelmas.

LABOR

Thomas Taylor . . . . Six days work.
Peter Evans . . . . Six days work.
Isaac Warner . . . . Six days work.
Jonathan Patterson . . . . Six days work.
Joseph Patterson . . . . Six days work.
Remember Wright . . . . Six days work.
Hezekiah Stratton . . . . Four days work.
Benoni Moore . . . . Four days work."

Thus encouraged, Mr. Belden bought out the John Clary heirs and set his mill on the old mill-dam. The old grist-mill was built in 1685, and in 1716, Stephen Belding rebuilt it. He and his sons held it until 1779, when they sold it to Aaron Whitney. In 1717, Jonathan Belding and his brother Stephen built a saw-mill below. Stephen was half owner. April 10, 1728, Stephen sells to his brother Jonathan "one half of a saw mill now standing on the mill brook and all that pertains thereto, as also the whole privilege of the stream at that place, so that it be not prejudicial to the grist mill above; it being understood that this sale include only that side of the brook on which the saw mill stands." This mill was operated by Jonathan Belding, senior and junior, "as long as the old man was able to hoist a gate." Jonathan, Sr., had several children, and among them a daughter, "Submit." She was engaged to David Keyes, of Western,

Massachusetts, and as the wedding-day was set for August, 1756, she went to Hatfield in the spring and bought a piece of beautiful fine red cloth for her wedding-dress. Then she wove a blanket, and about a week before the day brought down from the best chamber the wedding-gown and hung it, with the blanket, out in the air. There was much to be done in the house by the daughters in those early days, and she went about her work singing. Suddenly a shadow passed the window, and what was her distress to see an Indian walking off with her beautiful gown and blanket on his arm. She called to him and begged him to come back, but he only waved his hand and, grunting, "Ugh! very pretty," hastened toward the great swamp.

Jonathan married for his second wife the widow of Benjamin Doolittle, and at the death of Mr. Belding, at eighty-three, the widow was wooed and won by Japhet Chapin. Miss Mary Montague, of Granby, a great-grand-daughter of Madam Belding, gives this account of the marriage: "Madam Belding was then living with her daughter Lucy, wife of Simeon Chapin, a son of the bridegroom, who also lived in the same family. The children, on coming home from school one day, were told that granther and granny were about to be married. They did not understand what this meant, and as children in those days 'mustn't ask questions,' they proceeded at once to make an independent investigation of affairs. They found granny up in her chamber, where their mother was pinning a purple ribbon to her best cap, while granther was found sitting in state in the square room below, where he was soon joined by the minister. The children had a dim idea that to be married the two must be together, so they silently seated themselves near the grandfather to wait the course of events. In due time they had their reward. As the ceremony proceeded, the minister requested the bride to take off her glove, which, as was then the fashion, reached above the elbow. One of the little girls stepped forward and took it from her hand. When the proper time came to re-place the glove, she promptly arose and handed it back. By this means she got the name of 'Little Bridesmaid.'

"At the date of this marriage Mr. Chapin was eighty-two and Mrs. Belding was eighty. They were so strong that they rode from Chicopee to Northfield—forty miles—on horse-back without weariness. She was arrayed in a rich sky-blue camlet riding-hood made for the occasion. It is said that she possessed as great mental as physical ability, that she received an unusually fine culture before she was married, and ever after had the privilege of that class of society calculated to increase it. Her death in her ninety-second year was caused by a fall."

Janes's Island, named in early Massachusetts records, and then containing twelve acres, was "just above Pauchaug." It was granted in 1686 to Elder Janes. November 15, 1721, the island was sold to Stephen Belding, and is named in an old French map "Belding's Island." At that time it was wholly separated from the river bank, and the east channel deep enough to allow flat-bottomed boats to pass. It is now filled up and become a part of Doolittle's meadow.

January 10, 1724, Captain Kellogg writes to Governor Dummer, "I have fifty men committed to my care by Col. Partridge, forty of whom are at Northfield with me, and ten at Deerfield. These men I have with the utmost care kept watching and scouting. I would repeat my former request to yr Honor, with respect to our forts, yt some care might be taken yt they might be made better, for they are exceeding mean."

The Governor immediately directed Colonel Stoddard "to review the forts at Northfield, and advise and encourage the inhabitants to repair them."

Between this and the 5th of March, Stephen Belding's premises were surrounded by strong pickets and a heavily timbered mount built.

Jonathan Belding's account of work done at the North Fort:

Myself and team 1 day; and self and three cattle to cart .	£0 – 11 – 0
Five days work of self and sergt. Moor	0 – 12 – 6
Self and team to cart mount timber 1 day; and self one day's work at the mount	0 – 07 – 0
To 1063 feet of boards at 2s. 6d	1 – 07 – 0
To all the nails for the fort	0 – 10 – 0
To 2 hundred and a half ten penny nails Nathaniel Mattoons boards 863 feet, and 1 day to cart posts, and 2 horses 1 day, Jona. Janes board, 400 feet and 42 feet of plank.	
Dea. E. Mattoon 4 days' work at the fort and 320 feet of boards and one day's work with his oxen, 1 day's work at the mount, 1 day's work with his oxen to fetch in mount timber and 1 day's warding for a soldier which did work at the mount.	
Dekon Janes boards 600 feet; 1 day's work carting posts and 4 days' work at the mount.	
Joseph Petty, 6 days' work at the fort	0 – 15 – 0
and 292 feet of boards	0 – 07 – 0

The mounts were square towers, from fourteen to twenty feet high, and were made of heavy timbers, framed, and boarded up, with the upper story planked and fitted for a sentry.

FATHER RALLE'S WAR

1722–1725

Sebastian Ralle, or Rale, was of French descent, and was born January 4, 1657.   He was a Jesuit missionary to the North American Indians, and arrived at Quebec in October of 1689.

The Governor of Massachusetts said, in a letter dated January 19, 1725, " He (Ralle) instigated the Indians to war and rapine, instead of preaching peace and friendship, agreeable to the doctrines of the Christian religion—as is proved by the papers found among his effects at Norridgewock."

The war began June 13, 1722.   The people of Massachusetts bore the cost and did the fighting, and thereby obtained for the people of New England twenty years of peace. Although the war seemed to be between the people of Massachusetts and New Hampshire on the one side and the Indians east of the Merrimac River on the other, the real power against which the two colonies were fighting was the Governor-General of Canada and, through him, the King of France.

The death of Governor Vaudreuil, October 25, 1725, interrupted the Indian hostilities, and after much negotiation a treaty of peace was signed at Boston, December 15, 1725.

Not less than one-seventh of the men of Northfield were constantly in garrison or in active service from the spring of 1723 until the spring of 1726.   But peace was established, and lasted for twenty years.

Royal Denison Belden

In Father Ralle's War, on the muster-roll of Captain Joseph Kellogg's Company, November 20, 1723, to May 30, 1724, is found the name of Stephen Belding. He was among the number who "went up to ye great falls" on scouts, and who, among others, was referred to by Captain Kellogg in his journal.

CAPTAIN KELLOGG'S JOURNAL

"The first scout on November 30, 1724 went up on ye west side of Conn. River, and crossing ye west river went up to ye Great Falls, and returned making no discovery of any enemy. The second scout went up to West river, and following up ye river 6 miles, and then crossed the woods to ye Great Falls, and returned seeing no signs of ye enemy. The third scout went west from Northfield about 12 miles, then northward crossing West river and steering east came to the canoe place about 16 to 17 miles above Northfield.

"The fourth struck out northwest about 6 miles, then north across West river and so to the Great Meadow, below ye Great Falls, then crossed the Connecticut River and came down on the east side. This Meadow is about 32 miles from Northfield.

"The fifth, the men were sent up West river Mountain, there to lodge on the top and view morning and evening for smoaks, and from there up to ye Mountain at ye Great Falls and there also to lodge on ye top, and view morning and evening for smoaks.

- "The sixth went up to West river, which they followed five miles from the mouth of it which empties itself at ye foot of ye Great Falls and then they came down to the mouth of it and so returned. In addition, we watch and ward 3

101

forts at Northfield continually, besides what those 10 men do at Deerfield, and ye people are uneasy that we have no more men to keep ye forts than we have."

It was owing to Captain Kellogg that Northfield was not a third time destroyed. "By such vigilance and wear of soul and body was our village protected and our valley kept clean of blood."

1729. "A rate for defraying ye town and county charges levied on the Polls and Real and Personal Estates in Northfield Feb. 12, 1729. Tax on the Poll £0 3s. 9d—Jonathan Belden, Lieut Eliezur Wright, Zechariah Field and Stephen Belden paid the largest tax."

During the war men went to church fully armed, and even the call to public worship on the Lord's day was by beating the drum.

From 1726 to 1744 there was an interval of peace.

In 1731 Northfield made the first division of commons. Lot Number 47, containing thirty-seven and three-quarter acres, was Stephen Belding's.

February 19, 1736, Stephen Belding died. He and his wife Mindwell Wright had nine children, and it is not surprising that some of these children showed the same implacable hatred of Indians that distinguished their two grandfathers, Benjamin Wright and Stephen Belding.

In the old cemetery at Northfield:

"HERE LIES INTERED MR.
STEPHEN BELDEN
HE DIED FEB. 19, 1736
IN THE 47 YEAR OF HIS AGE."

THE OLD FRENCH AND INDIAN WAR

1744-1748

March 15, 1744, war was declared by France against Great Britain, and on the 29th Great Britain declared war against France. The direct result was, of course, a war in New England with the Indians. Canada had been warned a month before, and had therefore an advantage, and had for years been preparing for just such an outbreak. The frontiers of Massachusetts and New Hampshire were directly exposed and in bad condition for effective warfare. Unfortunately, the two colonies were not harmonious, and the course followed by New Hampshire was strange. Having acquired the territory, she refused to protect the inhabitants, and claimed that it was to the interest of Massachusetts to defend them. This war lasted until the treaty of Aix-la-Chapelle in 1748, although Indian hostilities scarcely ceased before the resumption of war in 1755.

THE LAST FRENCH AND INDIAN WAR

1755-1763

Great Britain found that her colonies could not be assured of peace until France should be subdued on the frontiers, so the English government called on the provinces to furnish men, to be under the command of the British officers. These companies were to march on the French possessions on the St. Lawrence, Lake Champlain, and Lake

Ontario.   The intermediate frontiers must take care of themselves.

This war, from May, 1755, to May, 1763, cost Massachusetts four million two hundred and seventeen thousand dollars. Great Britain refunded one and one-half millions.

Concerning the Twin Brothers
Moses and Aaron

Richard
1591–1655

Samuel
1629–1713

Stephen
1658–1720

Stephen, Jr.
1689–1736

Moses—Aaron
1726	1726
to	to
1826	1748

INSCRIPTION ON ROCK AT NORTHFIELD, MASSACHUSETTS

Cut in 1748 in memory of Aaron Belden, who was murdered by Indians

106.

IN 1744 the old forts at Northfield were in good repair and the new ones strong, but there was great want of ammunition.

In 1720, the year Stephen Belden, Sr., died, his twin grandchildren, Moses and Aaron, sons of Stephen and Mindwell, were born. During the interval of peace they grew up to be strong and sturdy, and were both in garrison at Northfield during the French and Indian War.

May 31, 1748, Captain Melvin and his men were returning from a scout. They were attacked by Indians and completely routed. Six were killed, and Sergeant Petty so wounded that his comrades arranged pine-boughs for him to lie on, and, setting up others as a wind-break, placed a cup of water near him and begged him to live until they should return with help. Word reached Northfield in the afternoon of the next day. Captain Stevens, with a force of men, started for the scene of Melvin's defeat. They found and buried the dead, but by some mischance missed Sergeant Petty. The men of Northfield, however, were not content to leave him to his fate, and a company of sixteen, among them Moses Belding, started on the 5th of June to find him. They were gone four days on horseback, and found the body and buried it.

July 22, Captain Leeds withdrew his company of Connecticut troops from Northfield. The Indians had their scouts out in all directions, and were immediately made aware of Northfield's lack of protection.

It was three o'clock on the morning of the 23d of July, 1748. The Connecticut troops had left Northfield the day before, and the occupants of the fort, at the head of the main street, were sleeping soundly.

Just before sunrise a single figure stole quietly out of the gate and walked quickly towards the south. It was a lovely morning. The sun as it rose threw varied lights on the great elm-trees and the dew on the grass glistened like diamonds. The young man laughed low to himself, thinking how surprised and delighted his mother would be to have him breakfast with her. A shadow passed over his face as he thought how much happier he would have been if Moses, his twin brother, could have left the fort.

Moses and Aaron Belden were twin sons of Stephen and Mindwell Belden, and from their birth had been inseparable. It was almost impossible to tell one from the other, and their devotion to each other was known for miles around.

He crossed the little brook and came to the ledge of rocks jutting out into the street. A shot rang out, and almost with the sting of the bullet he felt the grasp of an Indian. Recognizing him as a supposed friendly brave, Aaron pleaded for his life; but with a curse the Indian drew his knife, cut round the crown, and, putting one foot on his neck, tore the scalp off entire. Striking his hatchet into his victim's head, he ran to join the other savages.

As the shot rang out on the clear air of the morning the men rushed from the fort.

Moses reached his brother first, and the dying man was

just able to give the particulars, then lapsed into unconsciousness, and died as they carried him into the fort.

Some years after, during an interval of peace, three Indians came down the river in a canoe. They moored their boat, and, walking single file as usual, went into the tavern on the main street. They drank freely at The Inn, and one of them boasted that the last time he was in Northfield he had killed a man.

"I killed him," he said, "just by the rock on the street. His name was Belden." Then he proceeded to give so many details that mine host of The Inn, Moses Belden, could not doubt that the murderer of his brother was feasting under his roof. Saying to his wife, "Give them whatever they call for," Moses took down his shot-gun and went out of the house.

At dusk the Indians went down towards the river. They had some difficulty in untying their canoe, and, as it glided out into the stream, the moon shone directly upon them. Suddenly the report of a gun was heard, then all was still.

Later in the evening Moses Belden returned home and hung up his gun in the corner.

Did he shoot the Indians? I do not know; but three days afterwards an empty canoe drifted into the river bank.

An inscription in the face of the rock where Aaron fell, cut by Thomas Elgar, who died in Winchester in 1762, reads:

"AARON BELDEN
WAS KILLED
HERE JULY
THE 23, 1748."

When Oliver Wright, who was seven years old at the time of the occurrence, related it to Deacon Phineas Field, he said, " Moses was the true avenger of blood !"

For many years the children on their way to school would run past the rock, saying there was blood on it.

Sarah Chamberlain, the wife of Moses Belden, came also of fighting blood. Her father's certified record in the Colonial Wars covers a period of thirty-four years,—from 1724 to 1758. He was captured by the Indians September 25, 1725, while on a scout. He died at Northfield, November 7, 1780. The church records say he "left a good name behind him." He was the son of Joseph Chamberlain, a soldier of Hadley in King Philip's War.

On the alarm the 1st of September, 1754, the families that had settled on their farms left their exposed homesteads and sought shelter in the town or at one of the forts. The Wrights and Beldens went to Hinsdell's fort.

Moses Belden died in Winchester, New Hampshire, at the home of his daughter, Mrs. Amasa Burt, in 1826, at the age of one hundred years.

Concerning Augustus Belding

Richard
1591-1655

Samuel
1629-1713

Stephen
1658-1720

Stephen, Jr.
1689-1736

Moses
1726-1826

Augustus
1753-1831

Main Street, Greenwich Village

WAR OF THE REVOLUTION

April 19, 1775–April 19, 1783

FROM April 19, 1775, to July 4, 1776, the colonists resisted taxation without representation and defended their rights as English subjects. From July 4, 1776, to April 19, 1783, the colonists fought for their independence.

April 19, 1775.

"All that night the march of the minute-men from every town in Massachusetts, from Rhode Island, from Connecticut, and from New Hampshire, kept the country towns awake. Before morning on the 20th, before Gage's tired troops were ferried back from Charlestown to their barracks, an American army was at Cambridge. The intelligence had flown over the land that the English troops had fired on the Lexington militia, and with it had gone the news that the column had been driven back to Boston. The story grew as it went from province to province. . . . No fiery cross ever stirred a nation to more eager enthusiasm."—BRYANT, *History of the United States.*

When the Revenue Act was passed, most of the families in Northfield resolved to forego the use of tea and foreign goods and to return to the use of sage and red-root and homespun cloth. In 1771 the number of sheep owned in Northfield was four hundred and thirty-seven, and in 1777 there were two thousand one hundred and sixteen. The spinning-wheels and looms were repaired, and the young girls were taught to make and dye cloth.

The minute-men of Northfield had been in training since the fall of 1774, and the Lexington alarm reached Northfield about noon of the 20th. The long roll was beaten by Elihu Lyman, and before night Captain Eldad Wright with his company of fifty-one men were on their way to Cambridge.

AUGUSTUS BELDING

Augustus Belding, Northfield, Captain Eldad Wright's company, Colonel Williams's regiment, which marched, April 20, 1775, from Northfield and Warwick to Cambridge. Service, twenty-three days. Also, Captain Eliakim Smith's company, Colonel Jonathan Ward's regiment. Also, muster-roll dated August 1, 1775; enlisted April 27, 1775; service, three months twelve days. Also, Captain Moses Kellogg's company, Colonel Ward's regiment.

Company return (probably October, 1775), also order for bounty coat or its equivalent in money, dated December 23, 1775.

Thirty-one of the name of Belden are on record in the archives of Massachusetts alone as having fought in the Revolutionary War.

In July, 1776, Captain Samuel Merriman enlisted a company of five-months' men for an expedition to Ticonderoga. Both Moses and Augustus Belden were in this company.

Augustus Belding, son of Moses Belding and Sarah Chamberlain, was born in Northfield, January 13, 1753. At the

Lexington alarm, April 20, 1775, he marched to Cambridge in Captain Eldad Wright's company. He was a minuteman, and served in Captain Eliakim Smith's company, Colonel Jonathan Ward's regiment, and in Captain Kellogg's company of the same regiment.

In 1786 he bought a farm in Guilford, Vermont, and in the same year, November 23, married Desire Denison.

"Guilford, November ye 23rd, 1786, then was the ordinance of Marriage Administered to Augustus Belden and Desire Denison both of Guilford by me William Bigelow, Justice of the Peace."

Their eight children were born in Guilford, and early in the century moved to Fabius, Onondaga County, New York. He died there at the home of his eldest son, Augustus, August 20, 1831.

"WARRANTY DEED.
"28th day of March 1786

"Know all Men by these Presents:

"That I Rufus Fish, Yeoman, of Guilford in the County of Windham and State of Vermont, for the consideration of Seventy five Pounds lawful money 375 Dollars received to my full satisfaction of Augustus Belden Merchant of Guilford in the County of Windham and State of Vt. do Give, Grant, Bargain, Sell and Confirm unto the said Augustus Belden his heirs and assigns a certain piece of land lying and being in Guilford in the County of Windham and State of Vermont, and described as follows, viz:

"Bounded South on land of James Packer Jun: West on the Propogation Lot: Northerly on land of Phillip Franklin and Phillip Franklin Jun: and East on James Packer's land.

"To have and to hold the above granted and bargained premises with the appurtenances thereto unto the said Augustus Belden his heirs and assigns forever, to them and their own proper use, benefit and behoof. And also I the said Rufus Fish do for myself my heirs, executors and administrators, covenant with the said Augustus Belden his heirs and assigns, that at, and until the ensealing of these presents I am well seized of the premises, as a good indefeasible estate, in fee simple, and have good right to bargain and sell the same in manner and form as above written and that the same is free from all incumbrances whatsoever.

"And furthermore I the said Rufus Fish do by these presents bind myself and heirs forever to WARRANT AND DEFEND the above granted and bargained premises to the said Augustus Belden his heirs and assigns, against all claims and demands whatsoever.

" Witnesses

" JEDDEDIAH FREEMAN
" SAMUEL DENISON"

" WARRANTY DEED.
" 2d day of August 1793

" Know all Men by these Presents:

"That I Augustus Belden, Yeoman, of Guilford in the County of Windham and State of Vermont, for the consideration of Eighty-seven pounds, Ten Shillings lawful money received to my full satisfaction of Obadiah Dickinson of Northfield in the County of Hampshire and State of Massa-

116

Royal Denison Belden

chusetts do Give, Grant, Bargain, Sell and Confirm unto the said Obadiah Dickinson his heirs and assigns a certain piece of land lying and being in Guilford in the County of Windham and State of Vermont, and described as follows, viz:

"Bounded South on land of James Packer Junior, West on the Propogation Lot, North on land of Phillip Franklin Jun, and East on land of James Packer Jun—containing twenty seven & two thirds acres of land be the same more or less—as by deed executed to the said Augustus, by Rufus Fish, as may fully appear. To have and to hold the above granted and bargained premises with the appurtenances thereto unto the said Obadiah Dickinson his heirs and assigns forever, to them and their own proper use, benefit and behoof. And also I the said Augustus Belden do for myself my heirs, executors and administrators, covenant with the said Obadiah Dickinson his heirs and assigns, that at, and until the ensealing of these presents I am well seized of the premises, as a good feasible estate, in fee simple, and have good right to bargain and sell the same in manner and form as above written and that the same is free from all incumbrances whatsoever. And furthermore I the said Grantor do by these presents bind myself and heirs forever to WARRANT AND DEFEND the above granted and bargained premises to the said Obadiah Dickinson his heirs and assigns, against all claims and demands whatsoever.

"Witnesses

"WM. BIGELOW
"ELIHU FIELD"

117

Ancestors and Descendants of

"March ye 5ᵗʰ 1787

"At the annual meeting of the inhabitants of the town of Guilford according to a notification Holden at The Widow Lucretia Houghton's in said Guilford were chosen

"JOB SALISBURY
"JOHN HEALEY
"EPHRAIM WHITNEY
"JOSEPH WEATHERHEAD
"ANDREW WILKINS
"EPHRAIM EDWARDS
"AUGUSTUS BELDEN
"JOHN CONNABLE

"*Haywards*

"Wᴹ BIGELOW

"*Town Clerk*"

"At the annual meeting of the inhabitants of the town of Guilford for the year 1788 the Inhabitants being met according to the warrant for that purpose at the house of the widow Lucretia Houghton—

"JOSEPH BULLOCK
"BENJAMIN CARPENTER
"STEPHEN CHASE
"PAUL CHASE
"DANIEL BOYDEN
"JOHN EDWARDS
"JAMES CUTLER
"JONATHAN ALDRICH JR.
"JOB WHITNEY

"SOLOMON BARROWS
"JOHN HAMMOND
"ISAAC THAYER
"JOHN NOYES
"DANIEL SMITH
"AUGUSTUS BELDEN
"NATHAN STARK
"DAVID GAINES

"*Were made Surveyors of Highways*

"Wᴹ BIGELOW

"*Town Clerk*"

Royal Denison Belden

"March 7ᵗʰ 1789

"Augustus Belden was re-appointed Surveyor of Highways and Samuel Belden, Paul Chase and Augustus Belden were appointed Fence viewers."

"In fact, my dear, you will find it a truly primitive state of society and if you have any adequate idea of the heartlessness of the world in general, you will rejoice in the friendly simplicity of these people among whom I have spent three or four of the happiest years of my life."—Royal Tyler to his bride when he brought her to Guilford, Vermont.

FROM ONONDAGA'S CENTENNIAL

By GENERAL D. H. BRUCE

"The original township of Fabius was No. 15 of the military tract. It was the home of the Onondagas. A portion of the town forms the great water-shed which divides the streams flowing north into the St. Lawrence from those which flow into the Susquehanna and other rivers on the south.

"The timber consisted of beech, maple, hemlock, ash, basswood, pine, oak, and valuable cedars. The entire town had a fine soil, susceptible of the highest cultivation.

"The first settlers of the town were a class of hardy, resolute men and women, endowed with noble traits, of New England parentage, and well qualified by nature to subdue a primitive wilderness. They brought to their new abodes unfailing courage and sterling characters, which they firmly implanted in the pioneer communities. It was these same attributes that subsequently brought so many prominent men of the

119

town into wider prominence and usefulness. The pioneers endured all the privations and hardships incident to a new country, but with true heroism mastered the situation and carved comfortable homes out of the dense forests. They were harassed by wild beasts and suffered from the prevailing miasma, and subsisted at times on game and such meagre supplies as distant markets afforded.

"With no roads save the parts marked by blazed trees, they lived in log cabins far from centres of luxury, yet the day came when the conveniences of civilization were brought to their very doors.

"Unfortunately, the town records prior to 1854 were burned in December, 1882. The tavern erected in 1814, known as the Cadwell House, is still occupied, and is owned by the Cadwell estate.

"Among the original twelve grantees of Fabius, soldiers of the Revolution, was John Cadwell.

"To this town in Central New York came Augustus Belden, and the farm on which he lived is still in the possession of the family."

Concerning Royal Denison Belden, his Children, and his Children's Children

.

Richard
1591–1655

Samuel
1629–1713

Stephen
1658–1720

Stephen
1689–1736

Moses
1726–1826

Augustus
1753–1831

Royal Denison
1795–1868

Royal Denison Belden
Born 1795

WAR OF 1812

1812—1814

*T*HE final cause of this war came from the fact that England kidnapped American seamen and forced them into military service. The government of Great Britain refused to stop the outrage, and for this reason Congress declared war in the summer of 1812.

ROYAL DENISON BELDEN

Royal Denison Belden, second son of Augustus Belding and Desire Denison, was born in Guilford, Vermont, February 17, 1795, and emigrated with his father and mother to Fabius, New York. He married, June 6, 1816, Olive Cadwell, daughter of John Cadwell.

In the war of 1812, Augustus Belding, Jr., eldest son of Augustus, was drafted. He had a wife and family, so his young brother, Royal Denison, insisted upon going as substitute. He was in garrison at Oswego, and was called the strong man of the garrison because of his prowess in wrestling.

It was a difficult matter at that time to obtain silver money in any quantity in the centre of New York State, so when the owner of a pair of horses which Mr. Belden wanted to buy asked for payment in specie, it necessitated a journey to Massachusetts on horseback. Mr. Belden brought back the money in saddle-bags, and the weight of it ruined the horse.

In 1827, Mr. Belden took his wife and two children to Pennsylvania, where he built a section of the Reading Canal. They were obliged to live in a Dutch family, and when the children returned to Fabius they were able to speak Dutch fluently. The family moved to Geddes in 1858, and Mr. Belden died there on July 2, 1868.

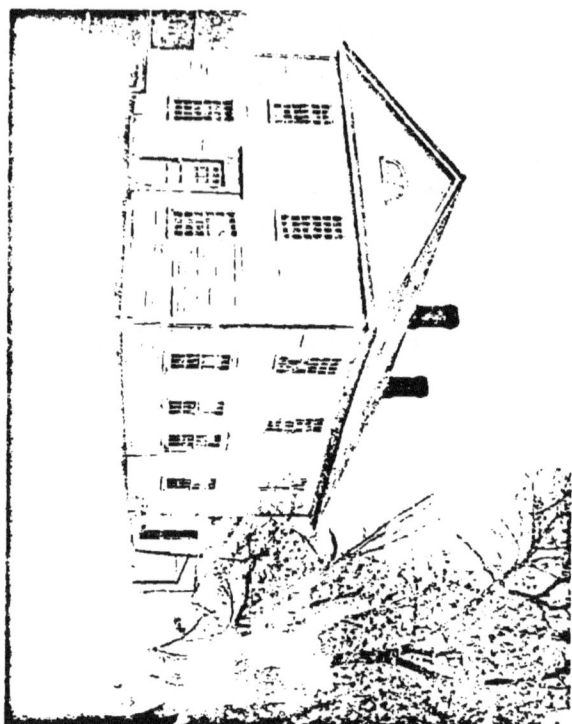

Augustus Cadwell Belden, Eldest
Son of Royal Denison Belden

A C Belden

Augustus Cadwell Belden
1897

AUGUSTUS CADWELL BELDEN

(Editorial, Syracuse Post, March 20, 1896)

"When a man dies who has been a good citizen, who has borne his part in life's struggles with courage, with integrity, with unswerving honesty and unsullied honor, society is the poorer at his departure. Such a man was A. Cadwell Belden, who died suddenly in this city yesterday. He had gone in and out before the people of Syracuse these many years, and they had learned to respect and admire him for those sterling qualities which give worth to true manhood. His life had been full of hearty endeavor, for he believed in the gospel of hard work. He had helped to carry forward large public enterprises, and to advance the material interests of the community in the development of its resources and in the promotion of public improvements. He had the rugged strength and genius for organization that are essential to large success in public work, and he did his part, not showily, but solidly and well. In his private life he was the unassuming, modest citizen, the kind neighbor, and loyal friend. He had held no political positions, but he was trusted by his fellow-men as one whose integrity and honor could always be relied upon. Those who knew him best loved him most.

"Augustus Cadwell Belden, eldest son of Royal Denison Belden, was born in Fabius, June 20, 1820. His grandfathers, Augustus Belding and John Cadwell, were among the pioneers of Onondaga County, coming from Massa-

127

chusetts and Connecticut early in the century. The old Cadwell house in Fabius, built in 1814, is still standing. Mr. Belden taught school in Fabius, and, June 23, 1841, married Rozelia Jackson, of Delphi.

"In 1854 he moved to Geddes, and in 1870 to Syracuse.

"Mr. Belden's first contract in the construction of public works was a portion of the Binghamton Railroad. Later he became a member of the firm of Denison, Belden & Company, and during a period of twenty years had large contracts in the United States and Canada.

"Mr. Belden was president of the Syracuse Solar Salt Company, president of the Cape Cod Salt Company, and was director in the old Water Company until the works were sold to the city.

"He built, and was for years general manager of, the Syracuse Northern Railroad, and also manager of the Chenango Valley Railroad. He was vice-president of, and with his brother, James J. Belden, founded, the Robert Gere Bank.

"Mr. Belden was president of the Board of Trustees of the First Presbyterian Church. He held many positions of trust, and was identified with the progress and welfare of Syracuse, where he had large investments in real estate."

From the Syracuse Standard

"Application was made in Surrogate Glass's court yesterday for the probate of the will of the late A. Cadwell Belden. All the heirs were represented and the will was admitted to probate. The application stated that at the present time it was impossible to place an accurate estimate on the value of the estate, the blank being filled out as 'unknown,'

128

Residence of Augustus Conwin Beld...
Syracuse, New York

Royal Denison Belden

but dispositions are so made that it will probably amount to over one million dollars.

"The document bears the date of December 5, 1893, and was witnessed by Edwin Nottingham and W. S. Andrews. The executors named are Alvin J. Belden, Frederick W. Barker, Martin A. Knapp, and John H. Moffitt."

RESOLUTIONS

"SYRACUSE, New York, March 23, 1896.

"At a meeting of the Counsellors of the Syracuse Home Association, held this day, the following resolutions were unanimously adopted:

"WHEREAS, The Syracuse Home Association has by the sudden death of A. Cadwell Belden been deprived of one of its most able and careful Counsellors; and

"WHEREAS, His associates have here assembled to briefly express and record our high esteem to our deceased friend;

"*Resolved*, That in all the various relations of life we have ever found our deceased friend and associate a kind, genial, pleasant, unassuming man, strictly honest, upright, and honorable; a man of great capacity, rare good judgment, and a cautious, careful, and safe Counsellor.

"*Resolved*, That in the death of Mr. Belden we have lost a good and true friend; his wife and sons, a kind and devoted husband and father; the Syracuse Home Association, an able and wise Counsellor, who always took a deep interest in its prosperity; the old ladies, a true and sincere friend; the Church, a consistent Christian gentleman; the charities, a substantial supporter; the poor, a generous giver who has done much to alleviate their sorrows and lighten their burden; the laboring man, a pleasant employer; the business men, a man of integrity and honor; the city, county, State, and nation, an honorable, honest, upright, and enterprising citizen. We hereby express our

9   129

deep sorrow for his loss, and extend to his family, in their hours of bereavement, our most sincere sympathy.

"*Resolved,* That these preambles and resolutions be entered at length upon the book of minutes of the Syracuse Home Association, a copy thereof printed in the daily newspapers, and a copy thereof presented to the family of our deceased friend.

"A. F. LEWIS,
"*Secretary.*"

"UTICA, New York, April 28, 1896.

"MRS. A. C. BELDEN, Syracuse, New York:

"DEAR MADAM,—At a meeting of the Directors of the Central New York Telephone and Telegraph Company, held yesterday afternoon, a minute was made in the records of the deep regret of the Board at the sudden death of Mr. A. C. Belden, whose intelligent interest and prudent counsel were greatly relied upon in the conduct of the affairs of the Company, particularly in all matters relating to the Syracuse Exchange.

"The Secretary was instructed to inform the family of the deceased of this action and to express the sincere sympathy of the Directors with them in their bereavement.

"Very respectfully,

"F. G. WOOD,
"*Secretary.*"

Citizens' Club of Syracuse

"At a meeting of the Board of Directors of the Citizens' Club the following resolutions were adopted:

"WHEREAS, The death of A. Cadwell Belden has removed from the membership of the Citizens' Club a respected and honored member, and as a testimonial of our deep regard for the memory of the deceased, be it

"*Resolved*, That this Club unites in lamenting t⊦
the death of Mr. Belden, the community, as well ₣
his social and business acquaintances, have met. A man of superior
executive and business ability, always true in his friendships, his
sudden demise is a great shock to his intimate associates in this Club.

"*Resolved*, That this tribute be entered upon the records of this
Club and a copy be transmitted to the family of the deceased.

"**W. H. Horton**,
"*Secretary.*"

"Syracuse, New York, April 16, 1896.

"My dear Madam,—As Secretary of the Ragged Lake
Rod and Gun Club, it is my privilege to transmit to you a
copy of a resolution adopted at the meeting of the Club last
evening.

"**G. S. Hier**,
"*Secretary.*

"To Mrs. A. C. Belden."

"At a meeting of the Board of Directors of the Ragged
Lake Rod and Gun Club, held at the office of the Club on
this 15th day of April, 1896, all of the members of the
Club and the Board of Directors being present, the following
resolution was offered by Mr. E. F. Holden:

"Our associate and friend, A. Cadwell Belden, has been called to
the future world. His going was unexpected, though he had passed
the scriptural allotted time. His associates in the Club deem it proper
to put upon the Club records an expression of their sense of loss.
Every member of the Club would speak tenderly and affectionately
of their social relations with our departed friend. We deplore his loss
in consequence of these relations, but the serious consideration which
is addressed to us is that Mr. Belden has become a loss to the community in which he so long lived.

131

Royal Denison Belden

"Therefore we deem it more gracious to speak of him as a citizen than in the closer and more personal relations of friendship. It might seem egotistical for this inconsequential Club to suggest expression to a bereavement so universally felt. Mr. Belden was a useful citizen. He gave character to this city. He was earnest and patriotic in every matter that concerned the city which honored him and which he always sought to honor. As his associates, we tenderly deplore his loss; as citizens of Syracuse, we more deeply deplore the loss to the community.

"Appreciating that this action of our Board of Directors will tend little towards assuaging the grief of his beloved family, we extend to that family the fraternal hand of friendship, and to the community we express sympathy for our general loss.

"G. S. HIER,
"*Secretary.*"

"At a meeting of the Board of Trustees of Round Island Park, held in the city of New York, April 9, 1896, the following resolutions in regard to the death of their late President, Mr. A. Cadwell Belden, were adopted:

"*Resolved*, That this Board sincerely deplores the death of our associate and the President of the Company, recognizing that in his ability as an officer, his fidelity in the interests of our enterprise at all times, and his sterling worth as a man and a friend, we have, in common with his fellow-citizens in Syracuse and his family, suffered a loss which cannot be over-estimated.

"*Resolved*, That we tender to his family our heartfelt sympathy in their affliction.

"*Resolved*, That these resolutions be entered upon the minute-book, and a copy, suitably engrossed, be sent to his family.

"CHARLES A. JOHNSON,
" *Vice-President.*
"CHAS. A. MYERS,
" *Secretary.*"

J. J. Belden

James Jerome Belden

1872

James Jerome Belden,
Son of Royal Denison Belden

J J Belden

James Jerome Belden

1897

JAMES JEROME BELDEN

(*From Congressional Directory*)

"ⱧON. JAMES JEROME BELDEN, of Syracuse, New York, son of Royal Denison Belden and Olive Cadwell, was born in Fabius, Onondaga County, New York, September 30, 1825. He is a descendant of Richard Bayldon, of England, who settled in Wethersfield, Connecticut, in 1635, and was the progenitor of a family numbering among its members distinguished men of the Colonial and Revolutionary period both in civil and military life.

"His mother was a descendant of Thomas Cadwell, who settled in Massachusetts Bay Colony prior to 1650.

"Mr. Belden was educated in Fabius, and when a young lad became a clerk in a store in his native town, where he showed unusual business ability. At the age of twenty-five, Mr. Belden went to California, entering with keen insight a new and broader commercial career. In 1852 he returned East, settling in Syracuse, where he married Mary Anna, daughter of Robert Gere, becoming associated with his father-in-law in the construction of public works, and later with his brother, A. Cadwell Belden, and Dr. Henry D. Denison. Among the firm's most important contracts were the first street-railways of Detroit and other cities, the enlargement of the locks on the Welland Canal, the Syracuse Northern Railroad, a portion of the West Shore Railroad, the Croton Reservoir, the Hell Gate improvements, dredging

135

New York and other harbors, and improving the canals of the State.

"The Robert Gere Bank in Syracuse was founded by Mr. Belden and his brother, A. C. Belden, in 1880. He is trustee of the Oakwood Cemetery Association and trustee of the Syracuse University.

"In 1877, Mr. Belden was elected, by an unusual majority, to the mayoralty of Syracuse without his knowledge or consent. He discharged the duties of his office with a keen perception of the city's best interests.

"Elected by a large majority a member of the Fifty-first, Fifty-second, and Fifty-third Congresses, he declined nomination the following year, but was elected afterwards to the Fifty-fifth Congress.

"Descended both on the paternal and maternal sides from a long line of patriotic ancestors, Mr. Belden was greatly interested in the formation of the Order of the Founders and Patriots of America, eligibility for which requires descent in the father's or mother's male line from an ancestor who settled in this country prior to 1657, and through a line of patriots. He became a charter member, and was elected a Councilor of the New York society. Later, on the formation of the General Court of the Order by the societies of New York, New Jersey, and Connecticut, he was elected a Councilor-General. He is also a member of the Sons of the American Revolution.

"Mr. Belden's sterling integrity is well known in financial circles, and this, combined with his force of character and careful judgment, has won for him prominence in civil and social life."

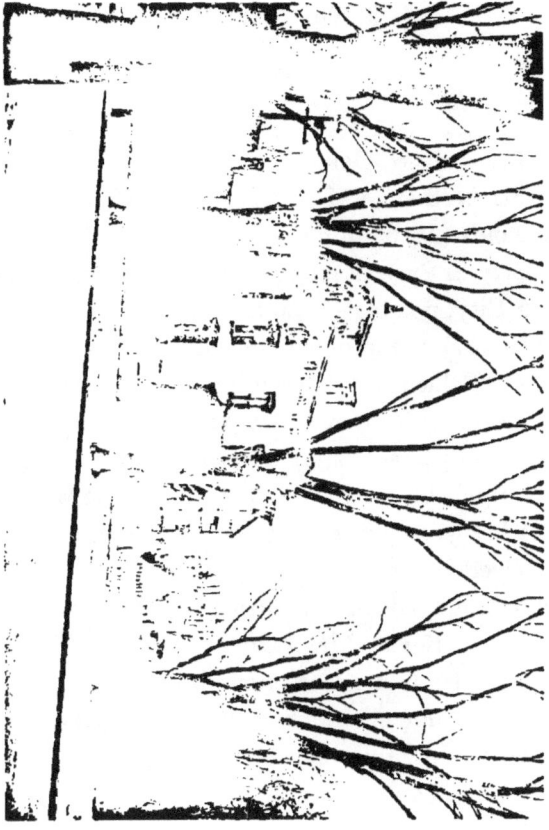

Royal Denison Belden

ONONDAGA'S CENTENNIAL

By GENERAL DWIGHT H. BRUCE

"The Robert Gere Bank, founded by James J. Belden and his brother, A. C. Belden, in 1880, moved into its present handsome building in 1894. In addition to his large property in Syracuse he has real estate investments in New York City, notably the Manhattan Hotel.

"In 1877 the people of Syracuse showed their confidence in Mr. Belden by nominating him for mayor without his knowledge or consent. He was elected by an unusual majority, and gained lasting admiration for the vigor and ability with which he discharged his duty. He was re-elected the following year by a very largely increased majority. He was elected to the Fiftieth and re-elected to the Fifty-first, Fifty-second, and Fifty-third Congresses, and then declined a renomination. Mr. Belden accepts criticism with good nature, defends his convictions with determination, has great force of character and tenacity of purpose, and is as well known for his quiet benevolence as for his political prominence and financial success."

MEAD BELDEN

Mead Belden, youngest son of Royal Denison Belden and Olive Cadwell, was born in Fabius, February 14, 1833.

At the time of his death, June 5, 1876, he was engaged with the various contracts of the firm of Belden & Denison. He married, in 1864, Gertrude, daughter of Gardner Woolson, of Geddes. Mr. Belden was Past Grand Commander of Knights Templar of New York State and Past

Eminent Commander of Central City Commandery. He was created a Sovereign Grand Inspector General of the 33° and Honorary Member of the Supreme Council by special commission of the Sovereign Grand Commander, in the city of Albany, on the 7th day of February, 1872, he having been duly elected at a previous meeting of the Supreme Council. His children, Edward Mead, Anna Louise (Mrs. Andrew S. White), Edith (Mrs. John Wilkinson), and Olive (Mrs. Henry Wigglesworth), reside in Syracuse.

ALVIN JACKSON BELDEN

Alvin Jackson Belden, eldest son of Augustus Cadwell Belden and Rozelia Jackson, was born in Pompey, New York, October 10, 1848. He was educated at Walnut Hill, Dr. Reed's school, Geneva, New York, and then became identified with the business interests of Syracuse. He is senior member of the firm of Belden & Seeley, contractors, and resides in Syracuse.

September 10, 1872, Mr. Belden married Augusta Pharis, great-great-grand-daughter of Mrs. Benjamin Pitney, who, after the battle of Monmouth, sheltered and clothed forty soldiers of the Revolutionary War.

JAMES MEAD BELDEN

James Mead Belden, son of Augustus Cadwell Belden and Rozelia Jackson, was born in Pompey, New York, July 10, 1852. He was educated at Walnut Hill, Dr. Reed's school, Geneva, New York, and at Cornell University. He was for a number of years in the wholesale lumber business, and is

138

identified with important interests in Syracuse. He was on the staff of General J. Dean Hawley, and later on the staff of General D. H. Bruce, with the rank of major, remaining with the brigade until it was transferred to Elmira.

He married, October 24, 1878, Jessie Perry Van Zile, daughter of Oscar E. Van Zile, of Troy, New York. They have five sons,—Mead Van Zile, James Jerome, 2d, Augustus Cadwell, Perry, and Oscar Van Zile.

CHARLES GILBERT BELDEN

Charles Gilbert Belden, youngest son of Augustus Cadwell Belden and Rozelia Jackson, was born June 6, 1857. He was educated at Bridgeman's school and Syracuse University. He is a successful contractor in Syracuse, New York.

He married, October 5, 1886, Mary Morrow Bevan, daughter of Dr. Thomas Bevan and his wife, Sarah Elizabeth Ramsey.

Dr. Bevan, son of Thomas Bevan, who came to Cincinnati from near Bristol, England, in 1818, was born June 11, 1831, and after graduating from the Medical College of Ohio finished his studies at the University of Paris, France.

He settled in Chicago in 1855, and was one of the founders of Rush Medical College, of the Medical Press and Library Association, of the Medico-Historical Society, and of the Society of Physicians and Surgeons. He was one of the surgeons at Fort Douglas during the Civil War. Among his published works are a series of monographs on "Sanitary Science."

Mrs. Belden is a grand-daughter of Elizabeth Dean, of

Parkersburg, Virginia, of Colonel George Ramsey, of Ohio, and great-grand-daughter of Jeremiah Morrow, the sixth governor of Ohio.

They have two children,—Arthur Bevan and Rozelia.

EDWARD MEAD BELDEN

Edward Mead Belden, eldest child and only son of Mead Belden and Gertrude Woolson, was born in Geddes, New York, April 16, 1865. He is a graduate of Williams College and a member of the Sigma Phi Fraternity.

He is private secretary to James J. Belden, and resides in Syracuse, New York.

Concerning certain Progenitors who did not bear the Name of Belden

ANCESTORS NOT NAMED BELDEN

AMONG the earlier settlers of New England whose descendants married members of this branch of the Belden family may be mentioned—

WILLIAM BEARDSLEY, of Stratford;
HENRY BURT, of Springfield;
RICHARD BECKLEY, of Wethersfield;
THOMAS CADWELL, of Hartford;
JOSEPH CHAMBERLAIN, of Hadley;
NATHANIEL DICKINSON, of Wethersfield;
NATHANIEL FOOTE, of Watertown;
THOMAS KILBORN, of Wethersfield;
WILLIAM HILLS, of Hartford;
RICHARD LYMAN, of Hartford;
EDWARD STEBBINS, of Cambridge and Hartford;
JOHN TAYLOR, of Windsor;
THOMAS WELLS, of Wethersfield;
HENRY WOODWARD, of Dorchester;
SAMUEL WRIGHT, of Springfield.

THOMAS WELLS was the son of Hugh Wells, of County Essex, England. He came to America in 1635, bringing his wife Frances and four children,—Thomas, Hugh, Mary, and John. He died in Wethersfield in 1640.

NATHANIEL DICKINSON, 1637, was the town clerk of Wethersfield and representative to General Court. He died in Hadley, June 16, 1676. Eighteen years later, just at sunset on the 14th of June, "a party of four Indians suddenly appeared in Hatfield North Meadow. They killed John Billings, aged twenty-four, and Nathaniel Dickinson's grandson, aged thirteen. They fired at his son, but missed him, killing his horse. A number of men and boys were taken captive, and the Indians took them away in canoes. Early in the night the news was carried to Deerfield just as a number of warm and weary troopers were returning from a two days' scout. Corporal Benjamin Wright, the grandson of Samuel, was among them, and they immediately turned their horses to the north, hoping to intercept the savages. After a hard ride of twenty miles they reached the Great Bend, opposite the mouth of the Ashuelot, just before sunrise. They halted and concealed their horses. In the distance they could see two canoes rapidly approaching. They waited silently until they could distinguish the faces of the Indians, then, taking careful aim, fired. One of the Indians was killed and the others, with one of the captives, jumped into the water. One boy remained in the canoe and the other turned to join him. An Indian tried to brain him with a hatchet, but received a mortal wound from the troopers. Neither boy was hurt, and they quickly paddled across to their rescuers. Three years after the murder of Nathaniel Dickinson, Jr., another son was born to Nathaniel and his wife Hepzibah. They named him Nathaniel, and, as if the name carried a shadow with it of tomahawks and scalping-knives, he also was killed by Indians, April 15, 1747." The following account of the killing of Mr. Dickinson was given in 1873 by his grand-daughter, Mrs. Polly

Holton, when she was ninety-three years old: " According to the town regulations, the meadows were pastured only in the fall, but owing to the fact that Indians were known to be lurking constantly in the adjacent woods in the autumn of 1746, the owners did not venture to drive their cows upon the Pauchaug Meadow. On the 15th of April, near sundown, Mr. Dickinson and Asahel Burt started on horseback to fetch the cows from the meadow. When going up Pauchaug Hill they were fired upon by the Indians. Dickinson's horse fell and he came down with it. Instantly the savages sprang upon him. As no guns were allowed to be fired except when Indians were discovered, the report of the fire-arms directly brought the people from Deacon Alexander's fort to the spot. Mr. Dickinson's eldest son, Ebenezer, was the first to reach him. Finding him still alive, he asked, 'Father, who shot you?' He answered, 'Indians,' and expired. The first intimation of the murder received by his wife was when the bleeding body was brought to her door. Soon after, the son whom she named ' Benoni' was born. He had from childhood the greatest dread of fire-arms, and could never be induced to use them. He could never listen to a tale of Indian warfare; and when drafted into the Revolutionary army, the officers, being informed of his inability to bear arms, assigned him a place in the commissary department. Even to old age he was never known to voluntarily speak of the death of his father." A rude stone was placed on the spot where Nathaniel Dickinson was killed. This has disappeared, but a few rods north a granite monument stands, which was dedicated at the field meeting of the Pocumtuck Valley Memorial Association at Northfield, Massachusetts, Thursday, September 12, 1872. It was erected by the great-grandchildren of Nathaniel Dickinson, and bears this inscription:

NATHANIEL DICKINSON

WAS KILLED

AND SCALPED

BY THE INDIANS

AT THIS PLACE

APRIL 15, 1747.

AGED 48.

NATHANIEL FOOTE married, in England in 1615, Elizabeth Deming. His children were born in England. In 1663 he received a grant of land in Watertown, Massachusetts. He died in 1644, aged fifty-one. His widow married, in 1646, Thomas Wells, magistrate, afterwards governor of the Colony.

Elizabeth Foote, wife of Daniel Belden, with her three children, Daniel, John, and Thankful, were "slaine by the enemie September 16, 1696, at Hatfield."

A bloodless tragedy, but one quite as interesting, is a part of the history of JOHN TAYLOR, who probably came to Windsor with the Rev. Ephraim Huit or Hewett, August 17, 1639. He was juror in 1641 and 1644. November 24, 1645, being "fully intended and prepared for a voyage for England," he made a will. In 1694 this will was presented for probate by John, son of the testator. Soon after his will was made, John Taylor set sail in the New Haven "Phantom Ship." In relation to this ship, which was never heard from except in the following manner, the Rev. James Pierpont, a Harvard graduate of 1681, minister at New Haven from 1684 to 1714, writes to Cotton Mather. This letter was incorporated in the "Magnalia," written 1695–96. "In compliance with your desire I now give you a relation of the apparition of a ship in the air, which I have received from the most credible, judicious, and curious surviving observers of it. In the year 1647, besides much other lading a far more rich treasure of passengers (five or six of which were persons of chief note and worth in New Haven) put themselves on board a new ship built at Rhode Island, of about 150 tons; but so walty, that the master (Lamberton) often said she would prove their grave. In the month of January, cutting their way through much ice, on which they were accompanied by the Rev. Mr. Davenport, besides many other friends, with many fears as well as prayers and tears they set sail. In June next ensuing a great thunder-storm arose out of the northwest; after which (the hemisphere being serene), about an hour before sunset a ship of like dimensions with the aforesaid, with her canvass and colors abroad (though the wind northerly), appeared in the air coming up from our harbor's mouth, which lies southward from the town, seemingly with her sails filled under a fresh gale, holding her course north and continuing under observation, sailing against the wind, for a space of half an hour. Many were drawn to behold this great work of God; yea, the very children cried out 'There's a brave ship.' At length crowding up as far as there is usually water sufficient for such a vessel, and so near some of the spectators, as they imagined, a man might hurl a stone on board her, the maintop seemed to be blown off, but left hanging in the shrouds; then her missentop; then all her masting seemed blown away by the board; quickly after the bulk brought into a careen, she overset and so vanished into a smoaky cloud, which in some dissipated, leaving, as everywhere else, a clear air. The admiring spectators could distinguish the several colors of each part, the principal rigging and such proportions, as caused not only the generality of people to say, *This was the mould of their ship*, and *that was her tragick end.*" Mr. Davenport declared in public that God had condescended, for the quieting of their afflicted spirits, this extraordinary manifestation of his sovereign disposal of those for whom so many fervent prayers were made continually.

HENRY BURT was born in England and came to Roxbury in 1639. He soon removed to Springfield, and was clerk of the band in 1640, and clerk of the writs in 1648. He died April 30, 1662. His son was in the party of scouts who rescued the Northfield captives.

WILLIAM BEARDSLEY was thirty years old when he came from England and his wife twenty-six. They came, with their three children,—Mary, aged four; John, aged two; and Joseph, aged six months,—in the good ship "Planter," 1635. It is supposed that they were in company with Rev. Adam Blakeman, of St. Albans, England. Hadley was their first home, then Hartford, and finally, about 1639, Stratford. Mr. Beardsley was elected deputy to General Court seven years. He died at the age of fifty-six. It is said that he came from Stratford-upon-Avon, and for that reason named the Connecticut town Stratford.

Royal Denison Belden

SAMUEL WRIGHT first appears in the town records of Springfield, Massachusetts, as juryman, December 12, 1639. He moved to Northampton in 1655, and was among the first settlers. He died October 17, 1665, "while sleeping in his chair." He was a descendant of John Wright, of Kelvedon, by his second son, John, of Wrightsbridge, County Essex, England. His son Samuel was a settler of Northfield in 1671, and with seven others was killed by the Indians at Squakheag, September 2, 1675.

Captain Benjamin Wright, father of Stephen Belding's wife, began his military career as corporal of the company in garrison at Northfield in 1706. As captain, his name was famous along the entire border. "His sagacity, strategic subtlety, vigilance, and knowledge of woodcraft enabled him to foil and outwit the Indians in their own peculiar artifices."

Massachusetts Archives: Military, vol. lxx. p. 384

"*To the Gentlemen Appointed to Grant Debenters or others who may be Concerned therein:*

"These may Inform that the Persons yt followed and way-laid the Indians: Redeemed o–r Captives; with the Loss of one and In probability of two o–r Enemies on the 14 of July 1698 Are As follows:

"*Benjamin Wright Corporall of the Troop: Leader.*"

*   *   *   *   *   *   *   *

Endorsed, "BENJAMIN WRIGHT, *Capten.*"

Massachusetts Archives: Military, vol. lxx. p. 386

"*To The Hono–bl Lieu–t Governo–r And Counsell and Repr–sentatives Now Sitting In Boston and*

"Tis Humbly Proposed by us whose Names are underwrit· ten In The Name of others with us: as are Here Inclosed:

whether upon the killing of The Indian after the Last mischief done by The Enemy at Hatfield we ought not according to the Law to be allowed fifty pounds: we did suppose the Law Continued untill peace was made with the Eastern Indians: wee have often ventered o—r Lives and had nothing upon sudden Exegencies we hope your hono— will Consider us and Alow the fifty pounds or at Least some other good Incouridgment: which will further oblige us to Venture o—r lives and estates for the Good of o—r Country.

" Benj Wright   ⎫ by the de-
" Jonath Taylor   ⎬ sire of the
" Benjamin Stebbins ⎭ Rest wt us:

" Ordered that *Benj—a Wright* be allowed three pounds, the six Inhabitants fourty shillings each and the seven Garrison Sould—s twenty shillings each to be paid them out of the Publick treasury.

" Nov: 29th 1698   In the house of Representatives
                  and sent up for Concurrence

            " Natha-l Byfield *Speaker.*

" In Council
    " Nov. 29, 1698 vot—d a Concurrence

            " Js—a Addington *Secry.*"

Massachusetts Archives: Military, vol. lxxi. p. 544

            " Northampton, Sept. 19th, 1709.

" *May it Pleas your Exel—y:*

            " With submishen and under Correction, I would offer my sarvise to your Exelency, if that in wisdome you send forces to Canada, from o—r Parts by Land, that here am I Send me, this year I have done sarvise, and hope I may again, not that I would troble your exelc—y, but am willing to goe, not else but in duty I subscribe your exelencys most Humble sarvant

" *Benjamin Wright*

" *To his Exelency Joseph Dudley Esed, Capt. genarel, and Commad-r in Chiefe: of the Provinc of the Masetchuset Bay, &c att Roxbury.*"
Endorsed, "Sept-r 1709 CAPT-N BENJ-A. WRIGHT *L-re.*"

Massachusetts Archives: Military, vol. lxxi. p. 595

"An accompt of Lost Goods by Severall persons in skirmishes pack horses and other services on Publique accompts as ffolloweth." . . .

" *Cap-t Benj Wrights* bill

" *Lost in his Late Expedition*

"To 1 blancket 10 gun case 1/6 hatchet 3/6
snapsach 2/6   0–17–6"

THOMAS CADWELL.

Thomas Cadwell located in Hartford, Connecticut, in 1652. He married, in 1658, Elizabeth, widow of Robert Wilson, and daughter of Deacon Edward Stebbins. They lived on a portion of Deacon Stebbins's home lot, on the corner of streets now Front and State. He was constable in 1662, and licensed to keep the ferry in 1681. He died October 9, 1694, leaving ten children. His estate was inventoried November 14, 1694.

WILL

"In the name of God, Amen, I Thomas Cadwell of Hartford in their Ma-is Colony of Connecticut in New England being well stricken in years and crasey in body, but through the mercy of God having the right use of my memory and reason and calling to minde the certainty of death and the uncertainty of the time, doe for the better settlement of my business in the disposeing of that portion of worldly goods which God in his holy providence hath left at my dispose. I do make this my last will and testament hereby revoking all other wills either by word or writing by me formerly made. I do therefore at my decease bequeath my immortall soule unto God in Jesus Christ who gave it my body I command to Christian Burial at the discresion of my executrix and overseers and my temporal estate after my just debts and funeroll charges are defrayed I give and bequeath as followeth I give unto my loveing wife Elizabeth the free use and improvement of all my whole estate whatsoever except what I have already given to my son Thomas, viz: that part of my home lot which he hath now in possession as it is already set out and fenced and improved by him for her to use and improve during her natural life also there is excepted that piece of land in the south meadow which was formerly my father Stebbins and by me given to my daughter Mary Dickins which she hath received and allready exchanged with Mr. Wm. Gibbon for land at podunck.

"I give unto my son Edward after mine and my wife's decease my lott in the long meadow near the landing place containing about one acre more or less lyeing between Mrs. Abigail Olcott and Mr. Nath: Stanley's lott and the reason why I give my beloved son Edward (he being my eldest son) no more is not out of any disrespect to him but because of that good estate his grandfather Stebbins gave him

which came to him in right of my wife his mother who was the only child living of his sayd grandfather when he deceased.

"ITEM. I give unto my son Thomas besides that part of my Home lot which he is allready possessed of all my lott in the long meadow containing about 4 acres lyeing between L–t Col. Tallcot and John Dayes lott allways provided the sayd Thomas relinquish his clayme to one acre and one rood of land in the south meadow thet his sister Mary Dickins may not be molested or troubled in that land in the South meadow that was formerly given to her. Allso I give unto him the one halfe of my grass lott at the lower end of the grass meadow lyeing between Mr. Lords and Thomas Olmsteds lotts allso my wood lott in the ox pasture lyeing between Lt. Col. Allyns land North, and John Skinner deceased his lot South and this he is to receive at the decease of me and my wife Elizabeth he paying his proportion of legacies to his sisters as shall be hereafter expressed.

"ITEM. I give unto my son Samuel the other halfe of my new dwelling house and halfe my barne and yards and home lot allso I give unto Samuel my lott at the upper end of the long meadow containing about six acres lyeing near Daniel Pratts lott allso the other halfe of my grass lott at the lower end of the long meadow the other halfe being bequeathed to my son Thomas. Allso halfe my wood lott in the West division of Hartford bounds the other halfe being bequeathed to my son Mathew and this he is to receive at the decease of me and my wife Elizabeth he paying his proportion of legacies to his sisters as shall hereafter be expressed.

153

"ITEM. I give unto my daughter Mary Dickins besides what I have given her formerly fower pounds to be payed in good current country pay of this colony and this is in consideration of fower pounds their grandmother Stebbins gave her at her decease she having allready received more than twenty pounds.

"ITEM. I give unto my daughter Abigail the just sume of Twenty pounds to be payd at the decease of me and my wife Elizabeth in good currant country pay of this colony.

"ITEM: I give unto my daughter Elizabeth the just sume of Twenty pounds to be payd at the decease of me and my wife Elizabeth in good and currant country pay of this colony.

"ITEM: I give unto my daughter Hanna the just sume of Twenty pounds to be payd at the decease of me and my wife Elizabeth in good and currant country pay of this colony.

"ITEM: I give unto my daughter Mehitabell the just sume of Twenty pounds to be payd at the decease of me and my wife Elizabeth.

"Further my will is that if any of my above sayd children that are yet unmarryed shall dye before they come of age without issue that their proportions allotted to them shall be equally divided amongst the survivors excepting that proportion which is given to Mathew. If he decease without issue then that my son Thomas shall enjoy it he payeing that proportion of legacies that is hereafter allotted to pay to the daughters (Mathew's legacy being mist in transcribing is here inserted it should have been entered before Sam'l legacy):

"ITEM: I give unto my son Mathew the one halfe of my now dwelling house and halfe my barne and yarde and home

154

lott remayning from that formerly given to Thomas allso my little pasture near the warehouse allso my lott called fordes lott in the long meadow containing about eighteen acres lyeing between Capt. Stanleys and Lt. Wadsworth's lotts also halfe my woodlot in the west division of Hartford Bounds and this he is to receive at the decease of me and my wife Elizabeth he paying his proportion of legacies to his sisters hereafter expressed.

"Allso my will is that my son Thomas upon the receiving his portion shall pay towards the legacies above sayd just five pounds in currant country pay of this colony allso that my son Mathew upon receiving his portion shall pay just thirty pounds in the same kind of pay allso that Samuel upon the receiving of his portion shall pay twenty pounds in the same kind of pay and the rest to make up my daughters legacies is to be paid by my executrix out of my moveable estate.

"Further my will is that what myselfe or my wife shall before death pay towards any of our daughters legacy aforesaid it shall be discounted off of their partes to whom it is payed and I do hereby appoint and ordaine my beloved wife Elizabeth my whole and sole executrix of this my last will and testament and do appoint and entreat my loving friends Mr. Nath. Stanley and Capt. Caleb Stanley to be overseers and helpful to my executrix in the fullfilling of this my will and for confirmation hereof I set to my hand and seal this 4th day of February, 1691.

"Thomas Cadwell.

"Witness :

    "John Pantry
    "Thomas Olcot."

"A CODSELL TO MY WILL

"Whereas in that clause of my will If any of my children under age or without issue &c., my will is that if any of my daughters be marryed before they dye that then their portion shall not return to the survivors allso my will is that my son Thomas shall have and enjoy the remaynder of that land in the south meadow which besides that which my son Edward enjoys and that which I have already given to my daughter Mary Dickins. As witness my hand this 11th day of February 1691.

"THOMAS CADWELL.

"Witness:
"THOMAS OLCOT
"The mark of E. C. of Elizabeth Cadwell Sen."

"May 25, 1694.

"Upon more deliberate consideration, I Thomas Cadwell Sen. doe make this further addition unto my last will and testament viz: I doe order and appoint my son Mathew Cadwell to pay unto my grandchild Wm. Cadwell ten pownds in currant country pay when he shall attayn unto twenty one years of age besides the twenty pownds I ordered him to pay towards his sisters legacies. I doe allso give unto my daughter Mary Digins Twenty Shillings besides the fowr pownds I have set down for her in my will. As witness my hand and seal the day and year above written.

"THOMAS CADWELL.

"Witness

"CALEB STANLEY SEN.
"SARAH STANLEY."

Royal Denison Belden

Deacon EDWARD STEBBINS, Cambridge, 1633; freeman Massachusetts, May 14, 1634. On committee to consider Endicott's "defacing the colors," May, 1635. An original proprietor of Hartford. Home lot in 1639 extended from meeting-house square to the street now Front Street. Constable in 1638. Deputy various times from 1637 to 1656. Leather sealer in 1659. Will dated December 23, 1673. Inventory August 19, 1668. Widow's will November 12, 1673. Both wills mention children. Only surviving child at the time of their deaths was the wife of Thomas Cadwell. Thomas Cadwell married in 1658 Elizabeth, widow of Robert Wilson and daughter of Deacon Edward Stebbins. Died October 9, 1694.

"Endicott's zeal under the influence of Roger Williams's teaching was made in an act of more moment than whether women should go without veils. The preaching of Williams was of the searching kind, and the application of his principles of undefiled religion knew no limit. There was in him no fear of principalities or powers; for the Church of England he had only abhorrence; for those who reverenced her, rebuke if not denunciation. In the red cross of St. George he saw only a remnant of Popery, not an ensign of victory. This fervid flame of pure spiritual doctrine caught up Endicott and he blazed into fury. When next the flag of England fluttered over him in the streets of Salem, he seized its folds and cut out the cross in which his pastor saw an emblem of submission to Rome. Some of the soldiers refused to follow the mutilated colors; the grave offence demanded the attention of the General Court; he was rebuked for indiscretion, and dismissed for a time from his seat as an assistant at the Council. It was only because all were persuaded that the act was done out of tenderness of conscience and not out of an evil mind that he was visited with no heavier penalty; and, besides, there were a good many people who sympathized with the act itself."—BRYANT, *History of the United States.*

WILL OF DEACON EDWARD STEBBINS

"HARTFORD August the 24th 1663.

"In the name and feare of God. I Edward Stebbins being weake in body but haveing my understanding and memory remaining with me through ye mercy of God yet not knowing the day of my death do here make my last will and testament. And I shall here speake only to ye things of this life w–h ye Lord hath bestowed upon me.

"FIRST: I give and bequeath unto my wel beloved wife Frances my howsing and lands in Hartford except such lands as are hereafter mentioned as appointed to be sold which shee is to enjoy for terme of her natural life, as allso two best cows three of the best swine as allso the use of the household stuffe or soe much of it as shee shall see need to make use of. Allso and in ye end of her natural life shee shall have liberty to dispose of forty pounds according as shee shall thinke fitt.

"ITEM: I give and bequeath unto our beloved son. John Chester the summe of forty pounds of my estate here to be paid w–thin two years of my decease my debts beinge paid: to be paid allso in this Countrey to him if he come at his arrivall over or to his assignes.

"Also. I give and bequeath after my wive's decease my housing and such of my lands as shall not be sold to pay

158

my engagements, I say I give them to Edward Cadwell my
son Cadwells child and John Willson and in case John
Willson should dy before he attayn ye age of twenty one
years y— the half of ye said house and lands I give to
Samuel Wilson at ye age of 21 years and if Edward Cadwell dy before he attayne ye like age then that halfe shall
pass to ye rest of my daughter Cadwells children and if John
and Samuel Willson should both dye before such age as aforesaid then ye whole shall pass to my daughter Cadwells children the one half to be equally divided amongst them.

"Allso I give to my son and daughter Cadwell for ye use
and benefit of their children ye sum of twenty pounds to be
paid in a feather bed and furniture such other household
stuffe or goods as shall seeme meet to my executors hereafter
mentioned to be paid within one yeare after my decease.

"Allso I give unto John Wilson a feather bed and furniture and such things as belong to my shop and trade. Allso
I give and bequeath to Samuel Wilson the sume of thirty
pounds to be paid that more y— is in William Phelps his
hands wch is to be prized quickly after my decease and the
rest to be paid out of other estate as the executors see good :
this estate to be paid to him at 21 yeares of age together with
the profit y— shall come of ye mare in wch regard he is to
stand to ye venture of the mare. Allso I give and bequeath
unto the four children of my deare sister Holyoke 40 / 8
apeace to be paid within one yeare after my decease excepting Johns part wch is to be paid when he shall attayne ye
age of 21 yeares.

"Allso I give to my son Gaylers children Joseph and
Benjamin and Joanna 8 pounds apeace to be paid into yr

fathers hands for yr use within two yeares after my decease and if eyther of his said children shall dy before they come to age viz: the sons to 21 yeares and ye daughters to 18 that part or parts shall pass unto the rest to be divided equally between them. Allso Mary Gayler I doe order to be with her grandmother I give unto her the summe of twenty pounds at 18 yeares of age provided shee carry it dutyfully to her grandmother, if otherwise it shall be in the power of my executors to abate according to yr discretion: Allso I doe appoynt that John Wilson shall be with his grandmother to helpe her accordinge to his best skill and ability during the term of her natural life and during wch tyme allso I desire my executors that care may be taken that he be instructed in my trade by Caleb Stanley according as it may stand with my wives comfort and after her decease I desire my executors to take order yt he be pfected in his trade And I do ordayne and appoint my well beloved wife to be my executrix of this my last will and testament Allso I do ordayne appoynt and desire honnor Samuell Willis and my well beloved brother and friends Elizur Holyoke, Lieut. Bull, Lieut. Robert Webster to be executors of this my last will and testament. To whom or to any two of whom I give power to see the legacyes above mentioned discharged and my just debts paid and to gather in wht debts are owing to mee and to make sale of wt of my stock is hereby undisposed of and if that will not satisfy to pay my debts then to sell that parcell of land yt I bought of Deacon Parke wch was Mr. Chaplaines lying up in the long meadow: about ten acres wth the lott and wt overplus shall be found of my estate after the legacyes above mentioned to be paid and my debts discharged after my wives decease shall be disposed of to my daughter Cadwells children and to John Wilson and Mary Gayler accordinge to ye judgement and discretion of my executors or any two of them: Allso I give to Richard Welles twenty shilings having formerly delivered into his hands about thirty pounds for the benefit of his children and to my said executors I give the summe of ten pounds viz: 50 / 8 apeace. And in witness hereto I have sett my hand.

" Edward Stebbins.

"This will and testament of Edward Stebbins was subscribed by him in ye presence of Elizur Holyoke."

Richard Beckley, whose grand-daughter married Matthew Cadwell, removed from New Haven to Wethersfield before 1668. He was the first English settler upon the land north of Mount Lamentation, in Meriden, part of the land belonging to the Mattabesett Indians and known now as "Beckley's quarter." There is a record of his title in the Wethersfield town records. He was also a lineal ancestor of Rozelia Jackson, wife of Augustus Cadwell Belden.

William Hills was an original proprietor of Hartford. His home lot in 1639 was on the corner of the highway, now Front and Sheldon Streets. He is supposed to have come in the ship "Lion" in 1632. He was constable in 1644, and then removed to Hoccanum. He was captain of the first train-band on the east side of the river, in 1653. In the colonial records of Connecticut, February 18, 1675, is the following: "The enemie having come to Hoccanum and shott at William Hill and sorely wounded him, the Councill sent forth a party of soldiers to make search for the enemie."

THOMAS KILBORN was born in England, probably at Wood-Ditton, in 1578. On the 15th of April, 1635, he with his wife Frances, and children sailed from London in the ship "Increase." They first settled in Boston.

RICHARD LYMAN, son of Henry Lyman and his wife Phillis, of High Ongar, County Essex, England, was an original proprietor of Hartford, Connecticut. In anticipation of his immigration to America he sold to one John Gower in 1629 "two messuages, a garden, orchard and divers lands arable, also a meadow and pasture" at Norton-Mandeville, in the parish of Ongar. He married Sarah, daughter of Roger Osborne, of Halstead, County Kent. In December, 1631, he arrived in Boston with his wife and children, Phyllis, Richard, Sarah, John, and Robert, in the ship "Lion" with John Eliot. They settled in Roxbury.

The following is in the handwriting of Eliot, and delayed Richard Lyman's admission as a freeman until June 11, 1633, for none but church members were entitled to the privilege.

"Richard Lyman—He came to New England in the 9th month 1631. He brought children—Phillis, Richard, Sarah, John. He was an ancient Christian but weake yet after some of tryal and quickening he joined the church; w—n the great remove was made to Connecticut he also went and underwent much affliction; for going toward winter, his cattle were lost in driving, and never found again; and the winter being cold and he ill provided, he was sick and melancholly; yet after, he had some reviving through God's mercy and dyed in the year 1640."

In 1636, in company with Revs. Thomas Hooker and Samuel Stone, he made the journey from Boston to Hartford, a journey of more than a hundred miles through the wilderness. They were but two weeks on the journey, although they had no guide but a compass.

A GENERAL COURT

November 15, 1644

" Richard Lyman hath the like liberty wth John Tynker and his p^rtners for the making of pitch and tarre pruided they gather not their wood w^thin halfe a myle of one another and that whatsoeur wood is or shall be gathered for that use be imprued w^thin three months after gathering."— *Colonial Records of Connecticut.*

ROYAL DESCENT OF RICHARD LYMAN

FROM THE SAXON KINGS

1. Cerdic, first King of the West Saxons, invaded England and established the kingdom of Wessex, where he reigned for thirty-three years, dying in 534. He was a descendant of Odin, who, according to tradition, lived the first century B.C.

2. Cynric, son of Cerdic, reigned twenty-six years, dying in 560.

3. Cheaulin, eldest son of Cynric, reigned thirty-two years. In 592 his throne was usurped by his nephew Cearlik, who

became fourth King of Wessex. Cheaulin died in exile in 593.

4. Cuthwin, son of Cheaulin, killed in battle in 584.

5. Cuth, son of Cuthwin.

6. Chelwald, son of Cuth.

7. Kenred, son of Chelwald.

8. Ingills, second son of Kenred.

9. Eoppa, son of Ingills.

10. Easa, son of Eoppa.

11. Alkmund, sometimes called Ethelmund, King of Kent.

12. Egbert, son of Alkmund, seventeenth King of the West Saxons, who succeeded King Bithric in 801. Married Lady Redburga, and died February 4, 836.

13. Ethelwulf, son of Egbert, married, first, Osburga, daughter of Oslac, his cup-bearer. Married, secondly, Judith, daughter of Charles II., the Bald, King of France. He died January 18, 857.

14. Alfred the Great, youngest son of Ethelwulf, born in 849, became king March 23, 872. Married, in 869, Alswitha, a daughter of the royal house of Mercia. He died October 28, 901. His wife died in 904.

15. Edward the Elder, son of Alfred the Great, became king in 901 and died in 925. Married, first, Eguina, a shepherd's daughter; secondly, Elfleda; thirdly, Edgiva.

16. Edgiva, daughter of Edward and his second wife, Elfleda, married Henry, third Count of Vermandois and Troyes.

17. Hubert, son of Edgiva, fourth Count of Vermandois, married Adelheld, daughter of the Count de Valois.

18. Lady Adela de Vermandois, daughter of Hubert, mar-

ried Hugh Magnus, fifth Count of Vermandois, son of Henry I., King of France, and grandson of Hugh Capet.

19. Lady Isabel de Vermandois, daughter of Lady Adela, married, first, Robert de Bellamont, Earl of Mellent, created Earl of Leicester by Henry I., of England. At the battle of Hastings he was characterized as "the wisest of all men betwixt this and Jerusalem in worldly affairs." He became a monk, and died in the Abbey of Preaux in 1118.

20. Robert, son of Lady Isabel and Robert, was second Earl of Leicester; married Amicia, daughter of Ralph de Waer, Earl of Norfolk.

21. Robert, son of Robert, third Earl of Leicester, surnamed "Blanchmains," died in 1190. He married Patronil, daughter of Hugh de Grentesmesnil, High Steward of England.

22. Lady Margaret de Bellamont, daughter of Robert, married Sayer de Quincey, one of the twenty-five barons selected to enforce Magna Charta. In 1207 he was created Earl of Winchester, and died in 1219.

23. Roger de Quincey, second Earl of Winchester, son of Lady Margaret, married Lady Helen, daughter of Alan, Lord of Galloway, and became in the right of his wife Constable of Scotland. He died in 1264.

24. Lady Elizabeth de Quincey, daughter of Roger, married Alexander, Baron Cumyn, second Earl of Buchan, a lineal descendant of the murdered Duncan.

25. Lady Agnes Cumyn, daughter of Lady Elizabeth, married Gilbert, Baron de Umfraville, eighth Earl of Angus, Governor of Dundee and Forfar Castles and the whole territory of Angus in Scotland. He died in 1308.

26. Robert de Umfraville, ninth Earl of Angus. He with William, Lord Roos, of Hamlake, and Henry, Lord Beaumont, was joined in the Lieutenancy of Scotland. He married, secondly, Alianore.

27. Sir Thomas de Umfraville, of Harbottle Castle, tenth Earl of Angus, son of Robert and his second wife Alianore, married Lady Joane, daughter of Adam de Roddam.

28. Sir Thomas de Umfraville, son of Thomas, born in 1364, Lord of Riddesdale and Kyme, married Agnes ——. Died in 1391.

29. Lady Joane de Umfraville, daughter of Sir Thomas, married Sir William Lambert, of Owton, in Durham.

30. Robert Lambert, son of Lady Joane de Umfraville and Sir William Lambert, of Owton.

31. Henry Lambert, son of Robert, of Ongar, County Essex.

32. Elizabeth Lambert, daughter of Henry, married Thomas Lyman, of Navistoke, County Essex. Died in 1509.

33. Henry Lyman, son of Elizabeth, of Navistoke and High Ongar, married Alicia, daughter of Simon Hyde, of Wethersfield, County Essex.

34. John Lyman, of High Ongar, son of Henry, married Margaret, daughter of William Girard, of Beauchamp, County Essex.

35. Henry Lyman, of High Ongar, son of John, married Phillis. Buried at Navistoke, April 15, 1587.

36. Richard Lyman, son of Henry, born in 1580, at High Ongar, removed to Roxbury in 1631, and died at Hartford, Connecticut, in 1640. Married Sarah Osborne.

DESCENT OF RICHARD LYMAN AND JOHN CADWELL.

FROM THE SCOTTISH KINGS

1. Kenneth I., called MacAlpine, 850–860.

2. Constantine I., son of Kenneth, 864–877. Killed in battle by the Danes.

3. Donald, son of Constantine, 889–900. Slain during the Danish invasion.

4. Malcolm I., son of Donald, 942–954.

5. Kenneth II., son of Malcolm, 971–995.

6. Malcolm II., son of Kenneth II., 1005–1054.

7. Bethoc, eldest daughter of Malcolm II., married Crinan, secular abbot of Dunkfield.

8. Duncan I., son of Bethoc, married a daughter of Siward, Danish Earl of Northumberland. During Duncan's reign (1034–1040) the Danes were joined by Macbeth, Duncan's cousin, who attacked Duncan, murdered him, and usurped the throne.

9. Malcolm III., called Canmore, son of Duncan, 1058–1093. Killed at Alnwick and buried at Tynemouth. He killed Macbeth and avenged his father. Married Margaret, eldest daughter of Edgar Atheling and great-grand-daughter of Edmund Ironsides, the King of the West Saxons.

10. David I., King of Scotland, son of Malcolm III., married Matilda, daughter of Waltheof, Earl of Northumberland, and Judith, niece of William the Conqueror.

11. Henry, Prince of Scotland, son of David I., married Ada, daughter of William de Warrene, Count of Warrene and Earl of Surrey.

12. Marjory, daughter of Henry, married Gilchrist, third Earl of Angus. Gilchrist donated to the Abbey of Aberbrothwick the churches of Moniford, Murrans, Kerimor, and Strachecton.

13. Duncan, son of Marjory, fourth Earl of Angus.

14. Malcolm, son of Duncan, fifth Earl of Angus, married Mary, daughter of Sir Humphrey Berkleykut.

15. Matilda, daughter of Malcolm, Countess of Angus in her own right, married, first, John Cumyn, who, in her right, became the sixth Earl of Angus; second, Gilbert de Umfraville, Lord of Prudhoe, Riddesdale, and Harbottle, Northumberland, who, in her right, became the seventh Earl of Angus. He was, according to Matthew Paris, "a famous baron, guardian and chief flower of the North." He died in Passion Week, 1245.

16. Gilbert de Umfraville, eighth Earl of Angus, only son of Matilda and Gilbert de Umfraville, married Lady Agnes Cumyn, daughter of Alexander Cumyn, second Earl of Buchan and a descendant of Donald Bane.

17. Robert, son of Gilbert and Lady Agnes, ninth Earl of Angus, appointed by Edward II. guardian of Scotland, married, secondly, Alianore ——.

18. Sir Thomas de Umfraville, younger son of Robert and Alianore, tenth Earl of Angus, succeeded by special entail to the castle of Harbottle and manor of Osterburn. Married Joane, daughter of Adam de Roddam.

19. Lady Joane de Umfraville, daughter of Sir Thomas, married Sir William Lambert, of Owton, in Durham.

20. Robert Lambert, son of Lady Joane de Umfraville and Sir William Lambert.

21. Henry Lambert, son of Robert, of Ongar, County Essex.

22. Elizabeth Lambert, daughter of Henry, married Thomas Lyman, of Navistoke, County Essex. Died in 1509.

23. Henry Lyman, son of Elizabeth Lambert and Thomas Lyman, of Navistoke and High Ongar, married Alicia, daughter of Simon Hyde, of Wethersfield, County Essex.

24. John Lyman, of High Ongar, son of Henry Lyman and Alicia Hyde, married Margaret, daughter of William Girard, of Beauchamp, County Essex.

25. Henry Lyman, of High Ongar, son of John Lyman and Margaret Girard, married Phillis ——. Buried at Navistoke, April 15, 1587.

26. Richard Lyman, son of Henry Lyman and Phillis ——, born at High Ongar, in 1580, removed to Roxbury, America, in 1631, and died at Hartford, Connecticut, in 1640. Married Sarah Osborne.

27. Phillis Lyman, daughter of Richard Lyman and Sarah Osborne, married William Hills.

28. William Hills, son of William Hills and Phillis Lyman.

29. Ebenezer Hills, son of William Hills, born in 1676; died February 12, 1749. Married Abigail ——; died in 1755.

30. William Hills, son of Ebenezer Hills, born June 16, 1702.

31. Abigail Hills, daughter of William Hills, born in 1737; died in 1744. Married John Cadwell.

32. John Cadwell, son of Abigail Hills and John Cadwell,

Royal Denison Belden

born January 9, 1758. Married Annar —— ; died March 3, 1839.

33. Olive Cadwell, daughter of John Cadwell and Annar ——, born February 25, 1794. Married, June 6, 1816, Royal Denison Belden.

Part II

Genealogical

Alvin J. Belden

1897 (see pages 138)

Genealogical

❦❦❦

LL historical and genealogical records in connection
with the line of Beldens

    1. RICHARD,

    2. SAMUEL,

    3. STEPHEN,

    4. STEPHEN, JR.,

    5. MOSES,

    6. AUGUSTUS,

    7. ROYAL DENISON,

have been certified. The genealogy of other Beldens is
printed as it was received, without verifying the records.

                J. V. Z. B.

BAYLDON . . . . . BELDEN

RICHARD BAYLDON[1] was born in Yorkshire, England; settled in Wethersfield, Connecticut, 1635; died 1655.

Children:

SAMUEL, born 1629.

JOHN, born 1631; married, April 24, 1657, Lydia ⎯⎯; was a trooper
of Wethersfield 1658; died 1677.

SAMUEL BELDEN[2] (Richard[1]) was in Hatfield 1673; died
January 3, 1713; married, first, Mary, who was killed in the

attack on Hatfield by Indians, September 19, 1677; secondly, June 25, 1678, Mary, widow of Thomas Wells (she died September 20, 1691); thirdly, Mary, widow of John Allis; fourthly, Sarah, widow of John Wells, April 10, 1704.

Children by first wife:

1. MARY, born July 10, 1655; married Daniel Weld, of Deerfield.
2. SAMUEL, born April 6, 1657; married, 1678, Sarah, widow of Samuel Billings; secondly, Mary, widow of Thomas Hastings.
3. STEPHEN, born December 28, 1658; married Mary, daughter of Thomas Wells, of Hadley, August 16, 1682. He died October 6, 1720.
4. SARAH, born September 30, 1661.
5. ANNA, born January 27, 1665.
6. EBENEZER, born November 16, 1667; married Abigail ——; had a daughter, Martha, born 1693.
7. JOHN, born November 13, 1669; married Sarah ——.

STEPHEN BELDING[3] (Samuel[2], Richard[1]), born December 28, 1658; married Mary Wells, August 16, 1682. He died October 6, 1720, and she married, January 2, 1723, Captain Joseph Field, of Sunderland, and died March 5, 1751.

Children:

1. ELIZABETH, born February 2, 1685; married Richard Scott.
2. MARY, born May 20, 1686; married, February 12, 1702, John Wait.
3. SARAH, born October 25, 1687.
4. STEPHEN, born February 22, 1689.
5. SAMUEL, born October 23, 1692; married, May 8. 1717, Elizabeth, daughter of Hezekiah Dickinson. of Springfield.
6. JONATHAN, born 1694.
7. JOSHUA, born 1696; married, December 1, 1725, Sarah Field. He died in Hatfield, 1738.
8. ESTHER, married, 1724, Nathaniel Gunn.
9. LYDIA, died July 24, 1714.

Residence of Alvin Jackson Tilden
Syracuse, New York

Royal Denison Belden

STEPHEN BELDING[4] (Stephen[3], Samuel[2], Richard[1]), born February 22, 1689; married, December 24, 1713, Mindwell, daughter of Captain Benjamin Wright. He died February 19, 1735–6.

Children:

1. LYDIA, born April 1, 1715.
2. THANKFUL, born January 6, 1718; married, 1741, Joseph Stebbins.
3. STEPHEN, born July 1, 1720; married, first, Abigail, who died January 5, 1764; secondly, Martha, from Hardwick. Thirteen children by first wife.
4. MARY, born July 9, 1722.
5. MINDWELL, born April 25, 1724.
6. MOSES, } twins, born February 23, 1726.
7. AARON, }
8. MARTHA, born January 19, 1727–8.
9. TITUS, born January 16, 1731–2; married, November 16, 1752, Anna Carew, of Springfield.

WILL OF STEPHEN BELDING

SON OF STEPHEN AND MINDWELL BELDING

"IN THE NAME OF GOD AMEN—

"I STEPHEN BELDING of Winchester in the County of Cheshire and State of New Hampshire, being of sound mind and disposing memory, do this twenty-seventh day of April, in the year of our Lord, Eighteen hundred and eight, make publish and declare the following as, and for, my last will and testament.

"*First:* I commend my soul into the hands of my Beneficent Creator, and my body to the dust, in the way of a decent Christian burial at the discretion of my Executors and humble hope that at the Resurrection of the just, I shall re-

175

ceive the same again by the mighty power of God and the worldly estate of which I am possessed I give devise and dispose of the same in the manner following—vizt

"I give and bequeath to my beloved wife, Martha Belding, the whole of my household furniture, to be at her sole disposal.

"I give and bequeath to the heirs of my daughter Hepsibah Wright deceased one dollar in full of her share of my estate.

"I give to my daughter Catherine Dean wife of Reuben Dean one dollar, in full of her share of my estate.

"I give to my daughter Mindwill Martindale wife of Elias Martindale, one dollar in full of her share of my estate.

"I give to my sons Stephen and Joab Belding one dollar each, in full of their share of my estate.

"I give to my daughter Martha Stebbins wife of Josiah Stebbins, Son deceased, One hundred and fifty dollars, in full of her share of my estate.

"I give to my daughter Hannah Smith wife of Samuel Smith Esqr—Two hundred dollars which will be in full of her share of my estate The above bequests I order to be paid (if demanded) in eighteen months after my decease by my Executor hereafter named.

"I give to my son Johnson Aaron Belding to be at his sole disposal all my wearing apparel, husbandry, tools, stock of cattle horses, sheep and swine. Also, I give to my said son Johnson Aaron Belding, the one half of all my real estate after my just debts funeral charges and legacies are paid.

"I give and bequeath to my beloved wife one quarter part of all my real estate after my just debts, legacies and funeral charges are paid to be at her sole disposal.

James M. Belden

1897 (see page 138

"I give to my grandson Stephen Johnson Belding son of my son Kerley Belding the remaining quarter part of my real estate after my just debts, funeral charges and legacies are paid.

"I humbly constitute and appoint my beloved wife Martha Belding and my son Johnson Aaron Belding sole Executors of this my last will and testament humbly empowering them or either of them, to sell such part or parts of my real estate (previous to any division thereof) as will be sufficient to pay my just debts, legacies and funeral charges and to give and execute good and sufficient deeds in law of the same. And the residue to be divided as above bequeathed. I hereby further give and bequeath to my executors jointly all my just dues and demands of what ever name or nature humbly ratifying and confirming this and none other as, and for my last Will and Testament.

"In witness whereof I hereunto set my hand and affix my seal the day and year above written.

"STEPHEN BELDING [L.S.]

"Signed, Sealed Published and declared by Stephen Belding as and for his last will and testament in the presence of us.

"JAMES SMITH
"ROBERT FLEMMING
"OBAD–H DICKINSON."

MOSES BELDING[5] (Stephen[4], Stephen[3], Samuel[2], Richard[1]), born February 28, 1726; married Sarah, daughter of Nathaniel Chamberlain.

Children :

1. **Dorcas**, born May 28, 1747.
2. **Annaretta**, born October 16, 1749 ; married, May, 1770, Amasa Burt.
3. **Augustus**, born January 13, 1753 ; married Desire Denison, November 23, 1786.   He died in Fabius, New York, August 20, 1831.
4. **Lydia**, born February 6, 1755.
5. **Rhoda**, born August 2, 1758.
6. **Moses**, born February 8, 1766.

Augustus Belding[6] (Moses[5], Stephen[4], Stephen[3], Samuel[2], Richard[1]), born January 13, 1753 ; married Desire Denison, November 23, 1786.   He died August 20, 1831.

Children :

1. **Augustus**, born July 1, 1788 ; married and lived in Fabius, New York.
2. **Desire**, born August 13, 1793.
3. **Royal Denison**, born February 17, 1795 ; married Olive Cadwell, daughter of John Cadwell, June 6, 1816.   She died February 1, 1856 ; he died July 2, 1868.
4. **Sally Maria**, born May 5, 1797 ; married James Jerome.
5. **Jabez**, born September 20, 1800.
6. **Edson**, born April 9, 1803.
7. **Merrett**, born June 2, 1806.
8. **Laura**, born April 12, 1809 ; married Mr. Stocking.

Royal Denison Belding[7] (Augustus[6], Moses[5], Stephen[4], Stephen[3], Samuel[2], Richard[1]), born February 17, 1795 ; married Olive, daughter of John Cadwell, June 6, 1816.   He died in Geddes, New York, July 2, 1868.   She died in Geddes, February 1, 1856.

Residences of James Mead Burden and of Mrs. *[illegible]*, Syracuse, New York

Children :

1. HARRIET, born September 27, 1817; married, January 28, 1834, David M. Benson. He died February 19, 1854; she died January 17, 1895.
2. AUGUSTUS CADWELL, born June 20, 1820; married, June 21, 1841, Rozelia Jackson. He died in Syracuse, New York, March 19, 1896.
3. JAMES JEROME, born September 30, 1825; married, October 25, 1853, Anna, daughter of Robert Gere.
4. MEAD, born February 14, 1833; married, July 5, 1855, first, Elizabeth Hubbell; secondly, March 31, 1864, Gertrude Woolson. Died June 5, 1876.
5. OLIVE, born November 14, 1835; lives in Oswego.

HARRIET BELDEN[8] (Royal Denison[7], Augustus[6], Moses[5], Stephen[4], Stephen[3], Samuel[2], Richard[1]), born September 27, 1817; married Dr. David N. Benson, January 28, 1834. He was a physician of prominence, and died February 19, 1854. Dr. David Benson was the son of Peter Benson, one of the pioneers of Onondaga County. Peter Benson was the son of Stutson Benson, who came to Pompey, New York, probably from Vermont, early in the century. Mrs. Benson died in Oswego, New York, January 17, 1895.

Children :

1. ELSIE A., born February 21, 1835; married Alanson Sumner Page, October 25, 1853; died November 14, 1896.
2. CADWELL B., born February 3, 1841; married, March 10, 1864, Helen J. Cunningham.

AUGUSTUS CADWELL BELDEN[8] (Royal Denison[7], Augustus[6], Moses[5], Stephen[4], Stephen[3], Samuel[2], Richard[1]), born June 20, 1820; married Rozelia Jackson, June 21, 1841; died March 19, 1896, in Syracuse, New York.

Children :

1. ALVIN JACKSON, born October 10, 1848; married Augusta Pharis, September 10, 1872; lives in Syracuse, New York.
2. JAMES MEAD, born July 10, 1852; married, October 24, 1878, Jessie Perry Van Zile ; lives in Syracuse, New York.
3. CHARLES GILBERT, born June 6, 1857; married May Bevan, October 14, 1886; lives in Syracuse, New York.

JAMES JEROME BELDEN[8] (Royal Denison[7], Augustus[6], Moses[5], Stephen[4], Stephen[3], Samuel[2], Richard[1]), born September 30, 1825; married Mary Anna, daughter of Robert Gere, October 25, 1853; lives in New York and Syracuse.

Child :

HARRIET, born July 21, 1858; died November 11, 1860.

MEAD BELDEN[8] (Royal Denison[7], Augustus[6], Moses[5], Stephen[4], Stephen[3], Samuel,[2] Richard[1]), born February 14, 1833; married, first, July 5, 1855, Elizabeth Hubbell, who died September 14, 1855; secondly, Gertrude Woolson, March 31, 1864. He died June 5, 1876.

Children by second wife :

1. EDWARD MEAD, born April 16, 1865.
2. ANNA LOUISE, born February 14, 1867; married, April 23, 1895, Andrew Strong White.
3. EDITH, born September 24, 1869; married, April 23, 1896, John Wilkinson. (Helen Wilkinson, born April 5, 1897.)
4. OLIVE GERTRUDE, born January 5, 1873; married, April 23, 1895, Henry Wigglesworth. (Silvia Wigglesworth, born July 8, 1897.)

ALVIN JACKSON BELDEN[9] (Augustus Cadwell[8], Royal Denison[7], Augustus[6], Moses[5], Stephen[4], Stephen[3], Samuel[2], Richard[1]), born October 10, 1848; married, September 10, 1872,

Chas. G. Belden
1897 (see page 139)

Royal Denison Belden

Augusta, daughter of Isaac Pharis; lives in Syracuse, New York.

JAMES MEAD BELDEN[9] (Augustus Cadwell[8], Royal Denison[7], Augustus[6], Moses[5], Stephen[4], Stephen[3], Samuel[2], Richard[1]), born July 10, 1852; married Jessie Perry Van Zile, daughter of Oscar Edward Van Zile, October 24, 1878; lives in Syracuse, New York.

Children:

1. MEAD VAN ZILE, born October 29, 1879.
2. JAMES JEROME, 2d, born December 5, 1881.
3. AUGUSTUS CADWELL, born October 11, 1883.
4. PERRY, born July 11, 1885.
5. OSCAR VAN ZILE, born December 4, 1888.

CHARLES GILBERT BELDEN[9] (Augustus Cadwell[8], Royal Denison[7], Augustus[6], Moses[5], Stephen[4], Stephen[3], Samuel[2], Richard[1]), born June 6, 1857; married May Bevan, daughter of Dr. Thomas Bevan, October 14, 1886; lives in Syracuse, New York.

Children:

1. ARTHUR BEVAN, born July 23, 1887.
2. ROZELIA, born August 31, 1894.

AUGUSTUS[7] (Augustus[6], Moses[5], Stephen[4], Stephen[3], Samuel[2], Richard[1]), born July 1, 1788; married ——.

Children:

1. HIRAM, married Nancy Austin, of Warren, Ohio. She now lives in San Francisco with her only son, Charles Belden.
2. JULIA, married John Schuyler.
3. EDWIN, married, first, Olive Williams; secondly, Olive Benson. Widow (Sarah) and daughter live in Fabius, New York.

4. JANE ELLEN, died unmarried.
5. CHARLOTTE, married Daniel Woodford.
6. CORYDON, died young.
7. WILLIAM E., married Phebe A. Colgrove. After his death she married a Mr. Kinney, and now lives in Syracuse, New York.

MERRETT[7] (Augustus[6], Moses[5], Stephen[4], Stephen[3], Samuel[2], Richard[1]), born June 2, 1806; married, February 25, 1829, Mary A. Schuyler; died March 16, 1871.

Children:

1. WARREN, born December 13, 1829.
2. OLIVE D., born October 10, 1831.
3. MARY, born June 6, 1833.
4. LAURA, born March 2, 1836.
5. WALLACE AUGUSTUS, born November 10, 1840.
6. ASHBEL K., born February 7, 1847.
7. SCHUYLER M., born May 14, 1851.

WARREN[3] (Merrett[7], Augustus[6], Moses[5], Stephen[4], Stephen[3], Samuel[2], Richard[1]), born December 13, 1829; married, March 16, 1853, Laura Connell; lives in Syracuse, New York. No issue.

OLIVE D.[8] (Merrett[7], Augustus[6], Moses[5], Stephen[4], Stephen[3], Samuel[2], Richard[1]), born October 10, 1831; married, January 1, 1852, Conrad Houck; died October 16, 1894.

Child:

LAURA ALMA, married, March 19, 1873, George T. Bradford. Their children are Grace Jerome, who married William H. Jago, June 24, 1896; and Frederick K.

MARY[8] (Merrett[7], Augustus[6], Moses[5], Stephen[4], Stephen[3], Samuel[2], Richard[1]), born June 6, 1833; married March 28, 1854; died without issue.

Edward Mead Belden
1877 (see page 140)

LAURA[8] (Merrett[7], Augustus[6], Moses[5], Stephen[4], Stephen[3], Samuel[2], Richard[1]), born March 2, 1836; married, December 29, 1852, Willard Sadler; died without issue.

WALLACE[8] (Merrett[7], Augustus[6], Moses[5], Stephen[4], Stephen[3], Samuel[2], Richard[1]), born November 10, 1840; married, May 26, 1886, Carrie Jerome. No issue.

ASHBEL K.[8] (Merrett[7], Augustus[6], Moses[5], Stephen[4], Stephen[3], Samuel[2], Richard[1]), born February 7, 1847; died January 7, 1848.

SCHUYLER M.[8] (Merrett[7], Augustus[6], Moses[5], Stephen[4], Stephen[3], Samuel[2], Richard[1]), born May 14, 1851; died September 30, 1864.

DESIRE[7] (Augustus[6], Moses[5], Stephen[4], Stephen[3], Samuel[2], Richard[1]), born August 13, 1793; married, November 3, 1815, Seth Wallace; died January 4, 1866.

Children:

1. JOSEPH W., born December 12, 1816; died March 22, 1843.
2. DENISON BELDEN, born September 15, 1818.
3. ZABINA H., born January 14, 1821; died April 11, 1895.
4. GEORGE W., born November 25, 1824; died August 16, 1877.
5. JOHN QUINCY ADAMS, born December 9, 1826; died April 17, 1843.
6. CHARLES, born June 14, 1830; died December 11, 1850.
7. B. F., born November 4, 1834; died January 21, 1853.

ZABINA H.[8] (Desire[7], Augustus[6], Moses[5], Stephen[4], Stephen[3], Samuel[2], Richard[1]), born January 14, 1821; married, first, Lucretia Fairchild, January, 1853; died April 11, 1895. No issue. Married, second, Hattie Seely Wallace, February 18, 1874.

GEORGE W.[8] (Desire[7], Augustus[6], Moses[5], Stephen[4], Stephen[3], Samuel[2], Richard[1]), born November 25, 1824; married, October 26, 1862, Catherine Griffith; died August 16, 1877.

Child:

ELLEN MAY, born June 25, 1868. She married, February 19, 1887, Sheridan E. Hughes, of La Grange, Indiana.

Issue:

HILDA WALLACE, born July 14, 1888.

SALLY MARIA[7] (Augustus[6], Moses[5], Stephen[4], Stephen[3], Samuel[2], Richard[1]), born May 5, 1797, married James Bishop Jerome; died September 17, 1867.

Children:

1. HENRY, born May 26, 1820.
2. GEORGE, born September 4, 1824.

HENRY[8] (Sally Maria[7], Augustus[6], Moses[5], Stephen[4], Stephen[3], Samuel[2], Richard[1]), born May 26, 1820; married, January 28, 1841, Elizabeth Schuyler. Living in Fairmount, New York.

Children:

1. EMILY, born June 18, 1842.
2. CARRIE, born August 20, 1844; married Wallace Augustus Belden.
3. SARAH, born November 2, 1846.
4. JAMES SCHUYLER, born April 20, 1849.

SARAH JEROME, grand-daughter of Sally Maria Belden, born November 2, 1846; married, February 20, 1873, Francis Dwight Parsons.

Children:

1. BESSIE, born March 11, 1874.
2. LAURA, born March 8, 1877.
3. CHARLES FRANCIS, born October 14, 1879.

4. BERTHA, born April 1, 1881.
5. JAMES JEROME, born April 19, 1884.
   Living in Syracuse, New York.

JAMES SCHUYLER JEROME, grandson of Sally Maria Belden, born April 20, 1849; married, September 27, 1876, Mary Amelia Parsons. Living in Fairmount, New York.
Children:

1. HENRY PARSONS, born October 4, 1877.
2. JULIA, born September 28, 1879.
3. EDWIN SCHUYLER, born February 8, 1884.
4. GEORGE WALLACE, born March 20, 1890.

LAURA STOCKING, daughter of Laura Belden (youngest child of Augustus Belden), born April 29, 1827; married, October 22, 1846, John Aumack.
Child:

WILLIAM J. AUMACK, born January 6, 1850; married, April 22, 1874, Sybil Kingsley.
Issue:

1. JOHN KINGSLEY, born January 23, 1875.
2. WILLIAM JAY, born November 18, 1876.
3. CHAUNCEY JEROME, born February 24, 1879.
4. JAMES SCHUYLER, born August 14, 1881.
5. LAURA BELDEN, born May 24, 1884.
6. LYDIA SYBIL, born August 5, 1887.

AUGUSTUS BELDING, OF WHATELY

JOSHUA (Stephen[3], Samuel[2], Richard[1]), born 1696; married, December 1, 1725, Sarah Field; died in Whately, Massachusetts, 1738.

JOSHUA (Joshua[4], Stephen[3], Samuel[2], Richard[1]), married Anna Fitch; died in Whately, 1805.

185

Royal Denison Belden

AUGUSTUS (Joshua[5], Joshua[4], Stephen[3], Samuel[2], Richard[1]), born 1773; married, 1802, Kate Weeks; died in Whately, 1816.

GEORGE W. (Augustus[6], Joshua[5], Joshua[4], Stephen[3], Samuel[2], Richard[1]), born 1804; married, 1826, Charlotte Robbins, and lived in Greenbush, New York.

CHARLES A. (George W.[7], Augustus[6], Joshua[5], Joshua[4], Stephen[3], Samuel[2], Richard[1]), born 1830; married Jennie Bassett; lived in Chatham.

"Belden, Samuel, son of Richard, had a daughter, Mary, and two sons, Samuel and Stephen, born to him by his wife, Mary, July 10, 1655, April 6, 1657, and December 28, 1658.

"Belden, Samuel, Jr., son of Samuel, married Hannah, January 14, 1685. They had issue, Samuel, born July 25, 1689; Daniel, February 14, 1691; Gideon, March 24, 1693; Prudence, February 12, 1694; Richard, April 18, 1699; Matthew, June 13, 1701; and Hannah, September 25, 1704.

"Belden, Samuel, first son of Samuel, Jr., married Mary Spencer, of Haddam, April 10, 1712. They had issue, Samuel, born April 26, 1713; Jared, January 19, 1715; Nathaniel, June 24, 1716; Lydia, May 24, 1718; Asa, April 1, 1720; Mary, December 11, 1721; Ann, November 7, 1723; Seth, September 18, 1725; Daniel, May 19, 1727; Richard, December 30, 1728; Phineas, September 14, 1730; Dorothy, September 6, 1732; Esther, June 22, 1734; and Martha, June 6, 1736.

"Belden, Daniel, second son of Samuel, Jr., married Margaret Clark, widow, daughter of Peter Blin, November 23, 1714. They had issue five daughters,—Margaret, Lois, Prudence, Eunice, and Thankful,—born September 10, 1715; June 14, 1717; January 28, 1719; March 17, 1722; November 10, 1724.

"Belden, Gideon, third son of Samuel, Jr., married Elizabeth, daughter of Zachariah Seimer (Seymour), February 7,

1712. They had issue, Eunice, Elisha, born July 22, 1715, Ruth, Elizabeth, Abigail, Hannah, Hezekiah, born October 26, 1725, Sarah, and Experience.

"Belden, John, presumed to be the second son of Richard, married Lydia, his wife, April 24, 1657. They had issue, John, born June 12, 1658; Jonathan, June 21, 1660; Joseph, April 23, 1663; Samuel, January 3, 1665; Daniel, October 12, 1670; Ebenezer, January 8, 1672; and two daughters, Sarah and Margaret. He was much employed in the public affairs of the town. He died in 1677, aged forty-six.

"Belden, John, Jr., son of John, married Dorothy, daughter of Josiah Willard, June 15, 1682. Had issue, Josiah, born February 14, 1683; John, December 3, 1685; Benjamin, 1687; Stephen, May 21, 1697; Ezra, November 27, 1699; and three daughters, Lydia, Hannah, and Dorothy.

"Belden, Josiah, eldest son of John, Jr., married Mabel, daughter of Sergeant Samuel Wright, May 1, 1707, and had issue, Josiah, born June 11, 1713; Oxias, November 18, 1714; Retrun, January 28, 1721; Solomon, May 22, 1722; and six daughters, Mabel Wright, Dorothy, Rebecca, Abigail, Lydia, and Hannah. Died September 5, 1746.

"Belden, John, 3d, second son of John, Jr., married Keziah, daughter of Sergeant Benjamin Gilbert, May 1, 1712. She died December 2, 1712, in premature childbirth, aged twenty-one. For his second wife he married Patience, daughter of Josiah Rossiter, Esq., March 22, 1715, by whom he had issue, John, born March 1, 1716. His wife died on the 9th of the same month, "aged 24 years wanting one month." He married for his third wife Sarah, daughter of Jacob Griswold, December 16, 1718, by whom he had issue, Ebenezer, born December 6, 1719; Timothy, December 26, 1723; and a daughter, Keziah, born August 21, 1722.

"Belden, Benjamin, third son of John, Jr., married Anne, daughter of Lieutenant Benjamin Churchill, January 29, 1714, and had issue, Mary, born December 9, 1715; Benjamin, February 9, 1718; and Charles, March 13, 1720.

"Belden, Ezra, fifth son of John, Jr., married Elizabeth, daughter of Deacon Jonathan Belden, February 15, 1722, by whom he had issue, Ezra, born November 29, 1722; Aaron, September 9, 1725; and a second Aaron, October 1, 1731; and three daughters, Elizabeth, Lois, and Eunice. From this family descended all the Beldens in Rocky Hill.

"Belden, Lieutenant, Esq., and Deacon Jonathan, second son of John, the first, was born June 21, 1660; married Mary, daughter of Thomas Wright, December 10, 1685. Had issue, Jonathan, born December 11, 1686; Mary, September 11, 1687; Silas, July 29, 1691; Jonathan, March 30, 1695; and Elizabeth, October 1, 1698. Greatly respected, and much employed in town affairs. He died July 6, 1734.

"Belden, Jonathan, his eldest son, died in childhood.

"Belden, Silas, his second son, married Abigail, daughter of Captain Joshua Robbins, November 30, 1716. Had issue, Silas, born November- 13, 1717; Abigail (married to Thomas Hurlbut, of Wethersfield), November 4, 1720; Joshua, July 19, 1724; Charles, May 4, 1726; Lydia, May 1, 1730; Oliver, November 19, 1732; and Jonathan, November 16, 1737. While he remained in Wethersfield he was much employed in public affairs. Disposing of his property in Wethersfield, he moved to Canaan in the spring of 1741, where he made purchase of large tracts of choice new land.

He made like purchases also in Dutchess County, New York, and in Berkshire County, Massachusetts, proposing to make them the future establishments of his children. In the autumn of 1741 he returned to Wethersfield to settle up his affairs and remove his family to his new possessions. At the time a malignant dysentery prevailed in Wethersfield. He was seized with it and died.

"Belden, Silas, Jr., his eldest son, settled in Canaan on a farm inherited from his father.

"Belden, Joshua, his second son, was liberally educated,—graduated at Yale College in 1743. He studied theology, was settled in ministry in Newington, November 11, 1747, and statedly discharged the duties of the sacred office until November, 1803,—fifty-six years. He married Anne, daughter of Lieutenant Ebenezer Belden, November, 1749, by whom he had issue nine daughters—Martha and Anne, both of whom died in childhood; Abigail, married to James Lusk, late of Enfield; Sarah, who died aged twenty-two; a second Anne, died in infancy; a third Anne; Martha, married to Joseph Lynde, druggist, late of Hartford; Octavia, married to the Rev. Nathaniel Gaylord, late of Hartland; Rhoda, married to the Rev. Silas Churchill, of New Lebanon, New York—and one son, Joshua, born March 29, 1768. His wife, Anne, died October 29, 1773. By a second marriage, with Honor Whiting, widow of Captain Charles Whiting, of Norwich, and daughter of Hezekiah Goodrich, Esq., of Wethersfield, November 14, 1774, he had a son, Hezekiah, born February 17, 1778. In 1772 he corrected the erroneous orthography of the family name, from Belding to Belden, at the suggestion of Colonel Elisha Williams, then town clerk,

the colonel showing him from the records an original signature of the first John, where the name was spelled as it now
is. He effected the change by addressing a circular, request-
ing the correction, to all of the name of whom he had knowledge, and it was at once very generally complied with, very
few thereafter spelling the name Belding, although there are
still a few who adhere to the corrupt spelling. [It would
have been better had he gone back one generation farther and
restored it to the correct spelling Baÿldon.] He died, July
23, 1813, in a good old age and ripe for eternity."

BIOGRAPHICAL SKETCH OF THE REV. JOSHUA BELDEN

*(From the Connecticut Evangelical Magazine and Religious
Intelligencer, November, 1813, vol. vi. No. 11)*

"He was born in Wethersfield, July 19 (O.S.), 1724. His
parents, Mr. Silas and Mrs. Abigail Belden, who sustained
the character of respectability and piety, were diligent in the
religious education of their son. This diligence was amply
compensated in his devotion to religion, and it affords encour-
agement to special care in teaching children to fear the Lord.
He was designed for a public educator. He commenced his
preparatory studies under the instruction of Rev. Stephen
Mix and finished them with a Mr. Williams, of whom he
used to speak with lively gratitude and complacency as his
patron and benefactor. He was admitted a member of Yale
College in 1739, was a diligent and sound scholar, and received his degree with reputation, 1743.

"He was an example of early attention to the religion of
Christ. In the second year of his collegiate course, as he

was laying the foundation for public usefulness in his literary attainments, divine grace, as he hoped, had a saving operation on his heart, and fixed his thoughts on the work of the Christian ministry.

"It was in the year of 1741, in the month of March, when he was in his seventeenth year, as he used to relate, that he first received those religious impressions which had a permanent effect on his mind. The circumstances of his first awakening were as follows: Having obtained leave of absence from the college for a few days, he rode to Wethersfield, in company with two or three of his fellow-students, on some special business among his friends. They left the college in high spirits, and their companions saluted them with jovial expressions as they departed. In their absence an astonishing change was wrought upon the college by a special religious awakening, which, like an electric shock, affected in a greater or less degree almost every member of the institution; but of this they heard nothing until their return. They arrived in town early in the evening, and expected to be hailed by their friends in the same spirit with which they had left them, when, to their great surprise, they observed a silence as solemn as the grave, and were unable to conjecture the cause.

"When he entered his room he found a number of his intimate acquaintances assembled, and beheld with amazement the change which three or four days had effected in their countenances and deportment. He could not forbear to ask what was the matter, when he was informed of the cause; and from this time it is understood that he made religion his supreme concern.

"This was the time when Whitefield and Tennent excited so much attention among the people, and when students were prohibited by the faculty of the college from going out to hear the preaching of those men. Mr. Belden and the celebrated David Brainerd were of the same class, but he was not a refractory subject, and did not believe that religion required him to disobey the authority of the college for the sake of hearing a particular preacher. He believed that the laws of propriety and religion were not hostile to each other.

"While he was a member of college his father, having sold his property in Wethersfield, and having made a purchase in Canaan, was cut off by death while making arrangements for a removal. His family, however, soon settled in Canaan. This event led Mr. Belden to relinquish the idea of his chosen profession and to turn his attention to the care of the bereaved family. At this time it was that the interposition of his friends assisted him in the decision which has given to the church the long and useful labors of this precious man of God. Dr. Hopkins, and another of the brethren in whose vicinity he then was, seeing the pressing call for ministers of Christ, and judging him to be eminently calculated for that work, went to reason with him on the course of life which he had taken. They found him at the plough. They urged upon him the point of duty, and persuaded him to leave the ordinary occupations of life for the work of preaching the kingdom of God.

"From this time he forsook all for his professional employment. After he had spent some time in his preparatory studies he was licensed to preach the gospel, and was recommended to the churches.

"He preached for some time in a frontier town, where alarms of Indians frequently disturbed the people, and where all the inhabitants used the precaution of sleeping within a fortification.

"When he had been a candidate about two years, he was invited, May, 1747, to preach in Newington; having preached to the people during several months, he was called to take the charge of them in the holy ministry. The people had employed a number of candidates in succession, but without union in their choice, and were at length happily agreed in Mr. Belden. After the various observations which had been made upon those which went before him, one of the leading characters was asked what he thought of Mr. Belden, and replied, 'An Israelite indeed.' He was ordained November 11, 1747.

"He was twice married; first, to Miss Ann Belden, next to Mrs. Honor Whiting. He had eleven children, six of whom died before him, and one since,—viz., Mrs. Martha Lynde, wife of Dr. Joseph Lynde, of Hartford. Four survive,—viz., Anne Belden, unmarried; the wife of Rev. Silas Churchill, of New Lebanon, New York; the wife of Rev. Nathaniel Gaylord, of Hartford; and Hezekiah Belden, Esq., of Wethersfield.

"Mr. Belden possessed 'a sound mind in a sound body.' His intellect was clear, his memory retentive, his judgment rational, and his mental exercises deliberate and firm. In his theology, which was his favorite, as well as his professional studies, he was a diligent and successful student. He acquired a clear understanding of the system of doctrine contained in the Word of God, and pos-

194

sessed firmness to defend them against the objections of the unbelievers.

"In the cultivation of those powers of mind he was employed from his childhood, and was favored with the best advantages of education which this country afforded at that time. He was a man of extensive reading, especially in the science of religion ; and this continued even to the close of his days. In this employment he spent most of his time after he left the active services of the ministry, and from long habit seemed unwearied in his application. His sight continued remarkably good to the last, in which he used to speak of the special goodness of God, as it furnished his mind with the employment and amusement of books.

"Another striking trait in his character was sobriety. His countenance bore that aspect of seriousness and gravity which was the true index of his mind. He maintained a dignified reserve in his deportment, which could not fail to inspire in the beholder respect and veneration, but which sometimes gave to strangers the idea of a man not familiar and easy of access. Levity and trifling, 'foolish talking and jesting,' were put far from him, and when he observed any conduct inconsistent with strict decorum of manners he frowned upon it as childish, 'unprofitable, and vain.'

"He was also distinguished for openness and sincerity. The sentiments of his heart were to be read in his expressions, which so plainly appeared as to remove insensibly from those who conversed with him even the suspicion of secret ambush and snares. To take in his companions by artifice and disguise, or to circumvent them, to show a knowledge of mankind and a power of managing them, was no part of that excellence of character to which he aspired. He was no flatterer, but treated every man according to his views of real worth, so that no room was left for an apprehension that an absent character would be traduced or injured by him.

"Temperance and frugality were prominent features in him. His bodily constitution was framed to stand against the revolutions of time, but it is proper to say his longevity was greatly owing to the strict rules of living which he observed. Of ardent spirits, if he drank at all, it was in a sparing manner, for he treated it as a dangerous thing. It was a principle with him that of the gifts of Providence nothing should be lost, but that everything should be turned to the best account.

"His speech seemed to be always with grace, seasoned in such a manner as to give a suitable answer to every man. Even his ordinary conversation was managed with great circumspection, correctness, and deliberation, elevated above low expressions, and might be assumed as a pattern of dignified discourse. He was ever on guard against descending to things which might strike any mind as improper in a man of his standing and profession. Indeed, he seemed always to speak under the impression that 'In the multitude of words there wanteth not sin.'

"He was a man of great regularity. His life was a life of method. Everything must be attended to in its place and order and with the utmost exactness. This rule ran through his ordinary business and through his professional labors. His mind was so constituted and his habits were so formed that to the last hour of his life his minute concerns must be adjusted in his accustomed manner.

Royal Denison Belden

"As a preacher of Christ he stood in the first rank. Well versed in the system of Christianity and deeply impressed with the weight of Divine truth, his conceptions were strong and his mode of expression was forcible. There was nothing splendid in his exhibition which might attract the attention of the curious and fanciful, but to those who are accustomed to estimate a preacher by his humble attachment to the gospel and an ardent concern for the salvation of men he appeared pre-eminently worthy. His great concern and his constant, recorded prayer was that the Word might be profitable to the souls of them that heard it. In preaching he depended much on the special Divine assistance, and enjoyed no satisfaction unless he supposed himself to have felt it in every discourse. After the Sabbath he used to describe the feelings of his heart in the exercises of the day, noticing his freedom with devout thankfulness and reflecting on himself with high severity for his cold and lifeless frames. His heart seems to have been on the work of the ministry, and every other concern appears to have been subordinated to this great design. The great truths which he believed and taught were the doctrines of grace. He honored and worshipped the Trinity of unity in God. He believed and felt that man in his fallen state has no moral goodness, but possesses the carnal mind, which is enmity against God and is dead in sins. The proper deity of Christ was with him a fundamental and essential truth. He received Christ as prophet, priest, and king. His only hope was founded on the Saviour's atoning blood. To this he directed sinners as the only foundation of eternal life. Salvation by grace was his delightful theme, and he often spake with great feeling of the all-sufficiency of

Christ. He renounced all dependence on works, and said that Christ was the only possible and the only desirable Saviour. He rejoiced in the eternal purposes, the sovereign government and electing grace of God. He believed as of infinite importance regeneration by the power of the Holy Ghost, repentance towards God, justification by faith, and complete salvation by Divine mercy. These things he impressed upon his hearers with ability, with affection, with zeal and fidelity. Had he been the immediate subject in Cowper's description of an apostolic preacher, it could not have been more exact:

> " '. . . Simple, grave, sincere;
> In doctrine, uncorrupt; in language, plain,
> And plain in manner; decent, solemn, chaste,

> " 'And natural in gesture; much impressed
> Himself as conscious of his awful charge.
> And anxious mainly that the flock he fed
> Might feel it too.'

"It is not too much to say that he was a man of extraordinary humility, for he neither attempted to exalt himself nor to pour contempt upon others. When he spake of himself it was in terms of dispraise, and when he spake of others he manifested a disposition to esteem them better than himself. He spake respectfully of all his brethren in the ministry, and even of young men he was ready to acknowledge that they could do better than he. In these respects a Mr. Belden is rarely to be found.

"He had a deep sense of sin and barrenness of life. While others looked upon him as a model of piety, his views of himself were extremely abasing, as appears most strikingly from his private writings, which were never calculated to be seen even by his own family. On the death of a minister who was his old acquaintance and special friend, he says, 'Why are the useful removed and I, an unprofitable servant, a burden to the earth, continued?' To give a more striking specimen: 'This morning,' says he, 'deeply abased, under a sense of my exceeding vileness and guilt, was enabled to pour out my mournful complaints of the wretched depravity and corruption of my nature, the numberless sins and most heinous offences of my life. Sins of youth and riper years, of omission and commission against God and man, stare me in the face. Oh, what a monster of rebellion, baseness, and ingratitude have I been! How have I buried my talents, as in the earth, a slothful servant! Oh, my negligence of my great work, pride, hypocrisy, earthliness, sensuality! God, be merciful to me, a sinner, who falls at the foot of a sovereign grace,—sovereign, almighty grace,—through a precious Redeemer. I was enabled to plead with fervent importunity.' Such were his habitual views of himself, and, though his crimes were invisible to others, yet to his last days he acknowledged to himself to have done nothing for Christ. He seemed to have uncommon views of the odiousness of sin, to groan under the burden of it, and to abhor it as abominable in the sight of God. 'I am assured,' said he, in conversation with a friend, 'I am assured of the universal and total depravity of my heart, of a total destitution of holiness or conformity to God. I know my own helplessness.'

"He had a high sense of the all-sufficiency of Christ for the salvation of sinners. While he felt his own helpless condition, he beheld in Jesus one who came to save His people from their sins, one perfectly adequate to the wants of the perishing soul. The Saviour appeared to him as the chiefest among ten thousand, and altogether lovely, and all his hope and consolation were in Him. 'I see,' said he, 'the sufficiency of Christ, and I think I find evidence of having cordially embraced Him. I renounce all creature dependence and look to Christ for justification freely by grace. Salvation is on no account a matter of debt; it is all grace. The atonement of Christ is such as lays a proper foundation for the pardon of the whole world, if they would come unto God by Him, and for the same reason that it is sufficient for the pardon of a single sinner.' 'I desire to give glory to God that the Gospel reveals an all-sufficient Physician, able and willing to heal and save. Were it not for this source of peace and comfort, my soul must sink in despair. Some intervals of light from this quarter keep alive a solacing hope amidst the darkness and disquietude that often hang over my mind. Oh, for deliverance from an evil heart of unbelief, for a more lively, active faith in the full atonement, the perfect righteousness of the Redeemer! Here is the only, the sure foundation of hope; here I desire to cast anchor for eternity. Yet, alas! how little, how weak my faith; how feeble and unsteady its exercises, if, indeed, I have any at all, and am not deceiving myself with the hope of the hypocrite which shall perish!' At another time he writes thus: 'If I am not deceived, I have an abiding, fixed hope and trust in Christ, His fulness, and the all-sufficiency of the atonement and righteousness that there is in Him, though too often mixed and clouded with distressing darkness, doubts, and fears, through remains of active or contracted corruption, which causes me often to cry out, "Oh, wretched man that I am, who shall deliver me from the body of this death? Thanks be to God for Jesus Christ. Whither shall I flee but to Jesus, the gospel refuge?"'

"He was eminently a man of prayer. This he considered as the great duty of the Christian life and the most important means of daily intercourse with heaven. Besides his ordinary seasons, he employed in self-examination and prayer the anniversary of his birth, the first day of the year, and other days which he occasionally separated for fasting and special exercises of devotion. On one of these occasions he writes thus: 'Oh, that I may be enabled wisely to observe and improve the dealings of Providence towards me and mine, and to conduct suitably thereto! Though I have repeatedly, and more frequently than usual, renewed my resolutions to be the Lord's since the commencement of the year, yet, alas! I find a law in my members warring against the law of my mind. The good that I would, I do not; but the evil that I would not, I do.'

"'*January* 1, 1762.—Through the wonderful goodness and forbearance of God I am brought to the beginning of another year. He hath taken one from my family and given another. Oh, that I might be taught to profit both by afflictions and mercies! and may the thought that I have one more year to account for and one year less to live have a quickening influence on my soul to greater diligence and fidelity in duty and fruitfulness in God's vineyard.'

"'*July* 30, 1782.—My birthday according to Old Style. May the Lord enable me to live more entirely to Him than

201

ever before. I determined to spend this day in reviewing my past life; in contemplating the Divine mercies to me; in calling to my mind my sins against God and my Redeemer with humiliation and prayer; and in renewing the surrender of myself and my all to Him as my God. The Lord guide my meditations, direct and fix my resolutions, and give me grace to spend and be spent in His service, and to fill up the residue of my days with usefulness and duty.'

"In prayer he manifested a distinguished fervor of devotion, a striking adaption of thought to the subjects, and a dignity and propriety of expression not commonly excelled.'

"Another thing to be noticed of him was his great love for the Word of God. This he read daily, for the direct purpose of personal devotion and spiritual improvement, in distinction from its use in the family and in his professional employment. 'If I am not greatly deceived, indeed,' said he, 'I can adopt the language of the Psalmist and of Job concerning the sweetness and preciousness of the Word of God. It is more precious than the most fine gold, sweeter than the honey-comb, and more important than my necessary food. It is my daily delight.'

"The Sabbath and public worship were peculiarly dear to him. On the day before the Sabbath he took care that every possible preparation should be made, so that the holy work of that day might not be interrupted by secular concerns. It was his care to preserve a serious and heavenly frame of mind through the day, and for this purpose he vigilantly guarded his thoughts, his speech, and his conduct. He was unwilling to receive company on the Sabbath, because it diverted his mind from these contemplations, in which he chose to be engaged, and he was exceedingly grieved whenever his pleasures of the Sabbath were interrupted. It appears to have been his constant practice to mark down the frame of mind in which he spent that holy day. His delight in public worship was manifested by his extraordinary diligence in going to the house of God during the last ten years of his life, when it was no longer necessary for him to attend, as the acting pastor, and when multiplied infirmities of age seemed to form a fair excuse for his absence. Sometimes, when his friends thought it improper to go out, and when he himself acknowledged that it seemed as though he could not, still his love for the place where the Divine honor dwells would prevail over the infirmities of the flesh, and he would return refreshed by the exercises and enlivened by the communion with God. He would say, 'I know not how few my Sabbaths may be, and I am unwilling that anything but necessity should deprive me of the public privileges of one, and I believe that necessity is often pleaded as an excuse when it does not exist.' He was more delighted in the performances of other ministers than his own, and often wrote animating accounts of the pleasure he found of the public service of his brethren. In the most uncomfortable weather, when almost all the people thought themselves excused from the house of God, he would be there; nor was he entirely prevented until within a few months of his death. The following extracts from his writings may give a specimen of his views and feelings on this subject: 'How amiable are thy tabernacles, O Lord of Hosts! Truly, a day in thy courts is better than a thousand. What a blessed institution is the Christian Sabbath! I find it good to me to draw near to

God and to wait upon Him in His sanctuary. Blessed be His name, for His Word, Sabbaths, and Sacraments, and for the continued and unmolested enjoyment of these precious privileges.'

" '*September* 17, 1809.—The Sabbath, as I get nearer the grave, grows sweeter, more delightful, more reproving and refreshing, and appears a most wise and gracious institution. Blessed be the Lord, that as yet I am able, with few interruptions, to seek and wait upon Him, in His sanctuary, on His holy day. Oh, may this precious season, and the ordinances of Divine worship be, indeed, more and more blessed, to prepare and ripen me for that rest which remaineth for the people of God in heaven !'

" Family religion, as it might have been expected of him from what has been said, was a privilege which he highly prized. He had his children in subjection with all gravity, and he was diligent to bring them up in the nurture and admonition of the Lord. His house was a house of prayer, and it was a matter of lamentation with him whenever infirmity made it necessary to omit the united worship of God in his household ; and urgency of business he would not admit as a good cause for neglect. But amidst all his decay, he was enabled to continue family prayer until within a day or two before his death.

" He was very particular in noticing the dispensations of Providence. It was a maxim with him to eye the Divine hand in every event.

" He was a man patient under affliction, and earnestly desirous that he might have a gracious operation upon his mind. Twice was he called upon to follow the desire of his eyes, and six times his beloved offspring, to the land of silence. In these and other tribulations he learned submission to the righteous providence of God. He passed through a heavy trial in the long distress and death of his first wife. In expectation of the event he thus prays: 'May God help me quietly to resign her into His all-gracious hand; and oh, that when the creature-streams are failing, my soul may have recourse to the infinite fountain and find a satisfying fulness in God!' She died October 29, 1773. 'Oh, how deeply does the arrow of Divine anger pierce my heart with grief! The desire of my eyes, my dearest creature-comfort, is taken from me now; but let me not repine, for it is God's sovereign right to take as well as to give. If earthly delights fail, if created streams are dried up, yet the fountain remains full. Oh, thither let me repair, and satisfy my mind! Blessed be God for so long an enjoyment of so dear and pleasant a companion. May the loss be made up in spiritual gain to me and my poor children. Oh, for Divine grace, that I may present to God the sacrifice of a broken and contrite heart, and come forth purified from the furnace of affliction; that I may mourn without repining, and so as to find comfort from a sealed pardon!'

"In the decease of his other wife it was his great concern that his mind and hers might be prepared for the event, and be submissive to the Divine will. 'May a gracious God accomplish his own work in and for her and bring her will cheerfully to submit to His, and prepare her and me for whatever that may be.' A short time before her death, when her mind was disordered, he said, 'Oh, that she might have the exercise of reason before she leaves us! if not, God's will be done, and may we submit and be fitted for that; only let her find mercy in the day of the Lord.' When her first son appeared, after a long absence, which was a day or two before her death, she seemed for a moment as if awaked from sleep, clasped him and cried, 'My child,' after which she took no more notice of him or of any other. She expired August 21, 1801, without a groan or struggle, and is gone, I hope, to perfect everlasting rest and peace. At this moment he said, 'It is God that hath done it; I am dumb and open not my mouth.' His after-reflection may be seen from the following example: 'How fleeting are creature-comforts! worldly joys how transient! What is a life? A vapor. Boast not thyself of to-morrow. To-day hear the voice of wisdom. Do with thy might what thy heart findeth to do. The Lord make me to know wherefore He contends with me, and let the fruit be the taking away of sin and making me a partaker of His holiness.'

"In May, 1808, his children being all removed from him, he left his own house and entered the family of his son, Joshua Belding, Esq., with the expectation of spending the remainder of his days with him. In a few days after his settlement in this family his son died, which overturned all his expectations. This was one of the greatest afflictions of his life. He bore it with calmness and resignation, which he had learned in a long life of trial. 'I had promised my-self,' said he, 'much comfort in that son, too much; God has wisely and graciously taken him away. I had looked upon him as the stay of my age and the support of declining years; but God is righteous and has right to rule and dispose of all His creatures. The Lord gave, and the Lord hath taken away; blessed be the name of the Lord. Alas! lover and friend have forsaken me, but Christ lives; God remains the same all-sufficient being.'

"His charitable donations, though concealed from principle while he lived, yet may now with propriety be brought into view. When he saw the needy he never sent them away empty. The indigent bless his memory. He felt a deep concern for the advancement of the Gospel kingdom, and gave liberally for the propagation of Christian knowledge. The writer of this article has been informed by a gentleman in the vicinity, who was made a secret agent in the business, that he had made an annual donation of ten dollars to the Missionary Society of Connecticut since the formation of that institution. In contributions his example was liberal. He did considerable in aid of the Tract Society of New Haven. He gave a hundred dollars to the funds of the Newington Cent Society, and fifty dollars to the Connecticut Bible Society.

"He was diligent in the employment of his time. He rose early in the morning and soon retired to his study, where he spent some time in devotions as a suitable introduction to the business of the day. Indeed, his study was his favorite spot. 'Here,' said he, 'is the place where I have enjoyed the greatest comfort, and where I have spent the greater part of my life.' Being in easy circumstances from the beginning of his course, he was enabled to command his time according to his pleasure, and also to furnish himself with whatever books he chose, a privilege in which he was distinguished above most of his brethren, who are condemned by the scantiness of their income to a dearth of books in the early part of their ministry, the very season when they are the best qualified to reap advantage from them and to prepare for more able ministrations to their hearers.

"He was able in council. The evidence of this is to be found in the multiplied instances of difficulty in which he was called to give advice, and from which it appears that none in his day had greater confidence reposed in them. And this confidence was well founded, for he had an ardent concern for the welfare of the churches, and his judgment was sound, as it was the result of experience and of conscientious thorough investigation.

"It is to be observed that he was a man of peculiar diffidence. Instead of showing to the best advantage, he always kept himself back, and placed more confidence in others than in himself, which concealed from the superficial observer many of the solid excellencies of his mind. This diffidence often subjected him to embarrassment in his public services, especially in the presence of strangers. We often find him abasing himself, and chastising in the severest terms his performances in other congregations than his own, and complaining of his 'old infirmity,' which it seemed impossible for him to surmount, and by which he was sometimes extremely depressed.

"He preached for the last time, and administered the Lord's Supper, November 6, 1803. During the ten years that followed it was an important work with him to give private warning and admonitions on the salvation of the soul as he had opportunity, and for this purpose he visited abundantly the dwellings of his people, and none who visited him were suffered to go away empty. He was a preacher of righteousness to the last, and was anxious to do all he could for the salvation of men. He had a colleague ordained January 16, 1805.

"He felt a strong concern for his country and for Zion, and this seemed to increase rather than abate as he drew near the close of his life. He was greatly distressed at the judgment which he saw hanging over the land, and prayed earnest and abundant prayers for the prosperity of the United States. He read with avidity the religious periodical works of the day, and was highly animated with the religious intelligence which he found; for nothing so delighted him as to learn of the revivals of religion and the diffusion of religious instruction.

"In these last years of his life he seemed to be engaged in nothing but preparation for eternity. 'As for the great event of death,' said he, 'it is every day in my thoughts; and though when I bring it nearest my nature seems to revolt, yet I have ordinarily no fears or terror at its approach. I desire to spend my whole time in contemplating futurity and waiting for the coming of my Lord.' His favorite books in his last years were the Bible, the abridgment of Henry on Prayer, by the North Consociation of Hartford County, and the Hartford selection of hymns. These lay constantly upon his table. The Assemblies Catechism was one of the greatest sources of comfort to him in his wakeful hours of the night, as it gave a lead to his meditations when his powers were so broken that he could not command and arrange his thoughts at pleasure. This he learned to repeat in his childhood, and retained to the end of his life, which he considered as a matter of special gratitude, as it furnished him with subjects of contemplation on all the important points of theology. He used to say that he often went through the whole of it in the course of the night.

"These are but faint notices of the man, whose examples shone as a light in the world, and whose removal has left a great vacancy in the church militant. One of the most aged and respectable ministers of the State being asked what character he would give of Mr. Belden, replied, 'I have ever looked upon him as a worthy, a good man, correct in his theological sentiments, and a pungent, powerful preacher.'

"It only remains now to give some account of the close of his life. It does not appear that he was ever visited with any hard or dangerous illness. In October, 1792, as he was standing about four feet from the ground for the purpose of gathering fruit, he received a shock which threw him to the ground, where he remained some minutes insensible. From this time he was afflicted with a vertiginous disorder which sometimes interrupted his public ministrations. About a year and a half before his death he was seized with a convulsion, which the physician thought to be apoplectic, and which was thought to indicate the manner of his death, but it proved otherwise.

"In September, 1812, that he might have everything in readiness to leave the world, he chose to make an arrangement of his temporal concerns, and accordingly distributed his property among his heirs, retaining such funds in his own hands and such a hold upon the whole as to give security and satisfaction to himself, and when he read the deed of confirmation, exclaimed, 'Now I am happy; I have done with the world.'

"He was confined at last but one day, and though he labored under infirmities more than he could name, yet he seemed to be affected by no bodily disease. His appetite was good till the last hour. The machine was worn out by time.

"Thursday morning, 22d of July, he was much exhausted by the exercise of rising. After he had rested a few moments he conversed freely. 'I have felt,' said he, 'greater comfort and satisfaction in religion these two days past than ever I did. There is an all-sufficiency in Christ. I rest in Him. He is my hope and happiness. I think I can say I know whom I have believed, and am persuaded that He is able to keep that which I have committed unto Him against that day. I pray God that I may not be deceived. I am willing to die. I long for it.' He passed that day and the next in quietness.

"*Friday, July* 23, 1813.—At evening he was asked whether he thought himself drawing near the close. He answered, 'I feel that I am gradually.' 'Are you content to leave the world?' 'Yes, though I am not wholly without my fears. There is a possibility of deception, yet I have such views as to raise me in good measure above its terrors.' To a neighbor he said, 'I am not able to talk much with you. I am glad that you have come to see me once more. I pray that God may be your teacher. One thing I would say to you: remember that the world will serve us but a little while, and there is an eternity before us, in which we shall be unspeakably happy or miserable, according as we spend our present time. I pray that God may make you experimentally acquainted with His truth and give you peace.' Then, taking him by the hand, 'So I bid you farewell.' After this he spake of the prosperity of Zion at large and, in a very feeling manner, of the state of our country. Of the millennium he said, 'I look upon it as near, but I do not expect to see it. I hope to be in a state more blessed than the millennium itself.' In about an hour he expired, and is, we trust, rejoicing in the presence of God. His mind was clear to the end. His sun set without a cloud."

FURTHER DATA FROM PAMPHLET BY R. R. HINMAN

"Belden, Joshua, Jr., eldest son of Rev. Joshua, graduated at Yale College in 1778; studied medicine and settled as a physician, and, after a few years, as a farmer, in Newington; married Dorothy, daughter of Lieutenant Lemuel Whittlesey, January 9, 1797; had issue four sons,—Lemuel Whittlesey, born January 6, 1801; Joshua, August 3, 1802; Chauncey, October 15, 1804; John Mason, August 26, 1806. He was highly esteemed, and died June 6, 1808, greatly lamented.

"Belden, Hezekiah, second son of the Rev. Joshua, was liberally educated, and graduated at Yale College in 1796; was a merchant in New Haven for some years; married Harriet Halstead Lyon, daughter of Underhill Lyon, Esq., of Rye, New York, December 28, 1818. Losing his wife, he removed to Richmond, Virginia, and, in connection with others, became a contractor for the transportation of the United States mail from 1823 to 1842, when he returned to Wethersfield, and is at present town clerk of Wethersfield. He has a son, George Huburtus, born October 12, 1819, who is now an engineer on the New York and Erie Railroad, and a daughter, Mary Honoria, born September 20, 1821.

"Belden, Lemuel W., eldest son of Joshua, Jr., graduated at Yale College in 1821; studied medicine and settled at Springfield, Massachusetts, as physician. He married Catherine, daughter of Stephen Chester, Esq., May 7, 1829; had issue a son, Donald, born January 21, 1831, who died June 1, 1837. Dr. Belden died, greatly lamented, leaving no issue, October 26, 1839. He was a man of great purity of mind, of amiable manners, and of rare attainments, and was rapidly rising into eminence.

"Belden, Joshua, second son of Joshua, Jr., graduated at Yale College in 1825; went to St. Louis, Missouri, and commenced business as a merchant; was unsuccessful; removed to Glasgow, Missouri, and retrieved his circumstances; married Agnes Morton Graves, daughter of —— Lewis, Esq., of Glasgow, a large landed proprietor, of the ancient family of the Lewises, of Virginia. He is now a landholder and farmer in Glasgow, has the unbounded confidence of the community about him, and has obtained the rare and enviable *sobriquet* of 'The Honest Man.' He has one surviving daughter, Elizabeth Morton, born April, 1838. His wife died two or three years since.

"Belden, Chauncey, third son of Joshua, Jr., was graduated an M.D. at Yale College in 1829; settled in West Springfield, Massachusetts, as a physician; married Lucy B., daughter of Justin Ely, Esq., of that place, November, 1834; had issue, Theodore, born June 8, 1836; Elizabeth, May, 1838; Chauncey Herbert, February 6, 1844; died in 1848. He was respected both as a physician and as a man.

"Belden, John Mason, fourth son of Joshua, Jr., married Mary Elizabeth, daughter of Mr. —— Hale, of Glastonbury,

213

June 14, 1838, and is settled as a farmer at Newington, on the old, ancestral Belden place. He has surviving issue, three daughters, Mary Elizabeth, Cornelia Hale, Agnes Whittlesey, born September 8, 1839; April 11, 1845; January 18, 1847.

"Belden, Charles, third son of Silas, was born May 4, 1728; settled at Dover, in Dutchess County, New York, on a fine farm inherited from his father. This family has furnished a member of Congress.

"Belden, Oliver, fourth son of Silas, born November 19, 1732; settled on a noble farm inherited from his father, in Lenox, Massachusetts. Two of his sons have been representatives of Lenox in the Massachusetts Legislature.

"Belden, Jonathan, fifth son of Silas, born November 16, 1737. Little is known of him by the compiler, not even his place of settlement. He undoubtedly shared with his brothers in his father's provident provision for his children.

"Belden, Jonathan, third son of Deacon Jonathan, born March 30, 1695; married Martha, daughter of John James, December 29, 1715; had issue, David, born October 4, 1716; Jonathan, March 8, 1719; Moses, December 29, 1720; and two daughters. He bore the military title of captain, was a justice of the peace, town treasurer a number of years, and much employed in public affairs. He died August 20, 1768.

"Belden, David, his eldest son, married Hepzibah Goodrich, August 3, 1769; had issue one daughter, born June 29, 1772.

"Belden, Joseph, third son of John, 1st, was born April 23, 1663, and married 'Mary his wife, October 27, 1693;' had issue, Joseph, born December 28, 1697; Thomas, Sep-

Colonel Thomas Belden Jr
Born 1732

tember 9, 1700; and four daughters, Sarah, Mary, Esther, and Eunice. It is supposed that Joseph died young, or left town, as there is no further mention of him.

"Belden, Thomas, second son of Joseph, married Mary, daughter of Rev. Stephen Mix (date of marriage not given); had issue, Thomas, born August 9, 1732; Joseph, November 4, 1733; and Simeon, February 24, 1737; and three daughters, Mary, Rebecca, and Lucy.

"Belden, Thomas, Jr., eldest son of Thomas, married Abigail, daughter of Dr. Ezekiel Porter, August 1, 1753; had issue, Ezekiel Porter, born February 12, 1756, and James, and two daughters, Mary (married to Frederick Butler, late of Wethersfield) and Abigail. He was liberally educated, and graduated at Yale College in 1751. He was highly esteemed, took an active part in public affairs, discharged the duties of many of the more important affairs of the town, and bore the titles of esquire and colonel. He died, May 22, 1782, greatly lamented.

"Belden, Ezekiel P., eldest son of Thomas, Jr., graduated at Yale College in 1775. The Revolutionary War had commenced, and he soon entered the service of his country as a lieutenant of light-horse in Sheldon's regiment. He continued in the service to the close of the war, and retired from it as captain with the honorary or brevet title of major. Subsequently he was colonel of militia. He married Elizabeth, daughter of Elisha Williams, Esq., September 26, 1781. By her he had issue, Abigail, married to Justin Ely, Esq., of West Springfield; Elizabeth, married to Daniel Buck, of Hartford; Thomas, born July 29, 1785, died February 24, 1831, without issue. His wife, Elizabeth, died October 30,

1789. November 1, 1790, he married Mary Parsons, of Amherst, by whom he had issue, James, born October 1, 1791, died September 13, 1800; Ezekiel P., born March 18, 1794, died April 2, 1818; Mary, married to Erastus F. Cooke, of Wethersfield; Celia, married to Heman Ely, of Elyria, Ohio; Julia, married to James L. Belden, of Wethersfield; Hannah, married to George Pryor. He was often and repeatedly chosen selectman; was elected town clerk in 1812, and held the office uninterruptedly until his death; was a member of almost all the town committees, a justice of the peace, and representative of the town in the General Assembly forty-nine sessions, and was elected to two more, in which he declined serving. He was a man of kind and social feelings, gentlemanly and amiable manners, and ready and active in the transaction of public affairs. He died October 9, 1824, honored and lamented.

"Mary[6] (Thomas[5], Thomas,[4] Joseph[3], John[2], Richard[1]), born —— ; married Frederick Butler, January 11, 1787; died January 17, 1811, aged forty years.

"Abigail Porter Butler[7] (Mary[6], Thomas[5], Thomas[4], Joseph[3], John[2], Richard[1]), born February 26, 1798; married, March 17, 1824, James Bidwell, of Utica, New York; died February 6, 1832.

"Esther E. Bidwell[8], born July 21, 1826. Abigail Butler Bidwell, born January 21, 1832; married Charles L. Cozzens, November 9, 1856; died June 7, 1892. Frederick Butler Cozzens, only child of Abigail Butler and Charles L. Cozzens, born May 15, 1860; died August 2, 1861. Miss E. E. Bidwell lives in the old Porter-Belden house, on Main Street, Wethersfield, Connecticut.

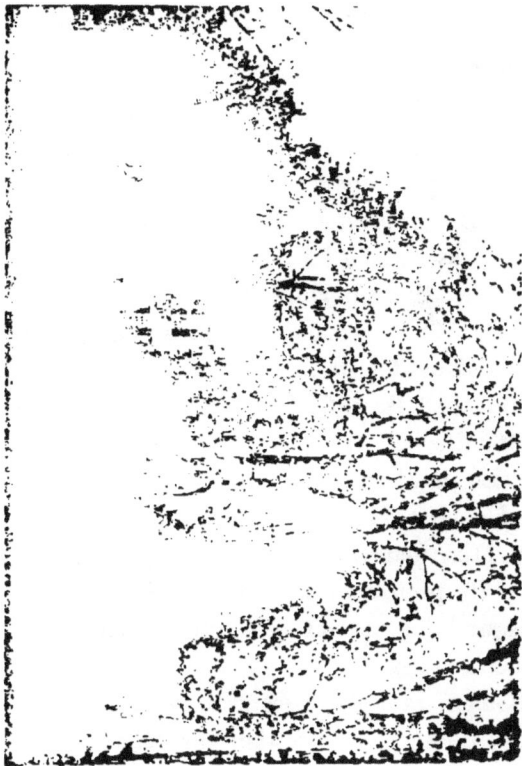

"Belden, Joseph, second son of Thomas, 1st, was born November 14, 1733, and graduated at Yale in 1751. It is presumed he removed from the town in early life, as his name does not appear again on the records or in the doings of the town. It is understood, however, that he had a son Thomas, who died at Hartford a few years since, leaving a family.

"Belden, Simeon, third son of Thomas, 1st, was born February 24, 1737; graduated at Yale College in 1762; married Martha, daughter of the Rev. James Lockwood, November 3, 1765; had issue, Simeon, born April 27, 1769 (settled at Fayetteville, North Carolina); Charlotte, married to the Hon. Lewis B. Sturges, of Fairfield; Martha, married to —— De Witt, Esq., of Milford; James Lockwood; Joseph; Mary Mix, married to Barzillai Deane Buck, of Wethersfield. By profession a merchant; held several of the town offices, and for several years was deputy sheriff. He died October 29, 1820.

"Belden, James L., second son of Simeon, was born October 15, 1774. By profession a merchant,—for a while successful, ultimately the reverse, and lost his property; turned his attention to horticulture, established the Wethersfield Seed Garden, and thereby retrieved his circumstances and accumulated a handsome property. Married Julia, daughter of Ezekiel P. Belden, Esq., September 28, 1819. By her he had issue three sons and one daughter. The eldest son and daughter died early in childhood. The survivors are Ezekiel P., born April 4, 1823, and James L., March 23, 1825. Ezekiel P. graduated at Yale in 1844, and is the ingenious modeller in wood of the cities of New Haven and New York. James L. has a spirit of enterprise and daring, and is a sailor on his first voyage. While at Wethersfield, Mr. Belden was held in high estimation and had much of the public confidence, and was an active and useful member of society. For a number of years he held the office of postmaster in the town. This he resigned to enable him to enter into the civil concerns of the State; was several times elected a representative of the town in the General Assembly, and was appointed a justice of the peace from year to year. In 1840 he removed to New Haven for the purpose of educating his sons. He was highly respected there. He was a man of sound judgment and of much shrewdness, conjoined with probity of character and great energy in action. He died in New York, February 22, 1847, and has his sepulture by the side of his fathers.

"Belden, Joseph, third son of Simeon, was born December 29, 1776; graduated at Yale in 1795; commenced business as a druggist, but after a few years became a general book agent, and by industry and tact made the business profitable both to himself and his employers; married Hannah, daughter of John Reynolds, of Enfield, November, 1813; had no issue, and died in 1826.

"Belden, Samuel and Daniel, fourth and fifth sons of John, 1st, born January 3, 1665, and October 12, 1670, it is supposed removed, the one to New London and the other to Norwalk (to his great-uncle William), and are the progenitors of the Beldens in those towns.

"Belden, Ebenezer, sixth son of John, 1st, was born January 8, 1672; no record of his marriage, but his son Ebenezer, by his wife, Abigail, was born September 7, 1697. He held at times nearly all the offices of the town, from hay-

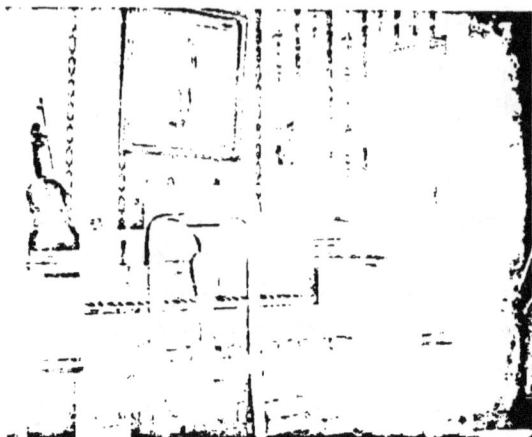

Interior Views, Porter-Belden House, Wethersfield, Connecticut

ward and constable to selectman, and bore the military title of sergeant. His son Ebenezer, born as above, married Mary, daughter of Coroner Samuel Talcott, December 7, 1720. Like his father, he held most of the town offices, and bore the military title of lieutenant. He had issue, Martha, born September 24, 1721, John, Anne (married to the Rev. Joshua).

"Belden, John, son of Lieutenant Ebenezer, like his father, ran the round of the town offices, and enjoyed the military title of colonel; married Rebecca Rennalls, June 12, 1760; had issue, Elizue, Rebecca, Mary, John, Ebenezer, Lucy, Ebenezer, Sarah, Nancy, and Harriet Man; time of his birth and death not recorded.

"Belden, Matthew, fifth son of Samuel, Jr., born June 13, 1701; married Elizabeth, daughter of Samuel Williams, April 16, 1729; had issue a daughter, Mercy.

"Belden, Samuel, 4th, eldest son of Samuel, 3d, born April 26, 1713; married Elizabeth, and had issue, Abner, born January 12, 1744; Bildad, September 9, 1745; Seth, August 7, 1747; Moses, June 18, 1749; and three daughters, Prudence, Rebecca, and Mary.

"Belden, Richard, seventh son of Samuel, 3d, born December 30, 1728; married Elizabeth Hurlbut, October 30, 1749; had issue, Amos, born October 26, 1750; Jeremiah, March 26, 1753; Othniel, March 27, 1755; Caleb, February 10, 1757.

"Belden, Phineas, eighth son of Samuel, 3d, born September 14, 1730; married Hannah Deming, March 22, 1751; had issue, Charles, born April 3, 1752, and a daughter, Mary.

"Belden, Aaron, third son of Ezra, born October 1,

1731; married Mercy, daughter of Matthew Belden, February, 1756; had issue, Moses, born August 14, 1756; Benjamin, October 25, 1757; Ashbel, September 18, 1759; Silas, December 28, 1761; Roswell, January 21, 1763; Justus, January 23, 1767; Aaron, September 14, 1769; and a daughter, Elizabeth."

"From the statement of CHESTER BELDEN, of Rocky Hill, Connecticut, a first cousin of Josiah Belden, said Chester being now dead several years. He said his father was a brother of Josiah Belden's father, and named Abraham or Abram. His paternal grandfather was Elisha, who died at Rocky Hill (or thereabout) in 1814. The children of Chester's paternal grandfather were Abram, Elisha, John, Joel, Josiah, 'Ziel,' whose real name he does not remember, and two daughters. The above statement was made by Chester Belden to Josiah Belden at an interview at Rocky Hill in October, 1884.

(Signed)   "LUIS F. EMILIO.

"NEW YORK CITY, December 13, 1896."

From the Statement of Josiah Belden, of San José, California, and New York City.

His father was Josiah Belden, who was born in 1777, probably at Rocky Hill, Connecticut, and who married Ruth McKee, also born in 1777.

Children:

1. ELIZA, born 1810 (who died a few years ago).
2. SUSAN, born 1813 (now living at Cromwell, Connecticut).
3. JOSIAH, born May 4, 1815 (who died April 23, 1892).

Royal Denison Belden

Josiah (the elder) died in 1829, and Ruth (his wife) in 1819. He died at Cromwell, where he had lived at least since his children were born. There was his home, and he had other property, being interested in vessels and shipbuilding. Having gone in a vessel in which he was interested from New York to Darien, he was taken with fever, and returning, the vessel put into Newport, where, from being taken ashore and exposed, he caught cold which developed into quick consumption, from which he died.

Memorandum from the Family Bible of Josiah Belden, of Cromwell, Connecticut, now in Possession of his Grandson, Charles Albert Belden, of San Francisco and New York City.

JOSIAH BELDEN, born April 16, 1777; died April 19, 1829 (at Cromwell, Connecticut); married Ruth McKee, of Cromwell, Connecticut, born June 17, 1777. She died August 12, 1819.

Children:

1. ELIZA M., born January 16, 1810; died July 14, 1891, at Cromwell. She married Otis Bowers.
2. SUSAN, born September 14, 1813; married, first, —— Stocking; and, secondly, ——. She is now living at Cromwell.
3. JOSIAH, born May 4, 1815.

NOTE.—From a manuscript record of the McKees in the family Bible of the Beldens, I find that Ruth McKee was the daughter of Joseph McKee, of East Hartford, Connecticut, born November 9, 1729, and Ruth Webster, born June 13, 1735. He died June 15, 1808, and his wife, Ruth, February 6, 1803.

Ancestors and Descendants of

JOSIAH BELDEN, born at Cromwell, Connecticut, May 4, 1815; died, New York, April 23, 1892; married Sarah Margaret Jones, at San José, California, February 1, 1849. She was born at London, Ohio, March 7, 1833.

Children :

1. CHARLES ALBERT, born March 6, 1851, at San José; married Fanny Hubbard, of Sacramento, California.

Issue :

1. CHARLES JOSIAH, born November 26, 1887, at San Francisco.
2. MARGARET, born September 25, 1890, at San Francisco.

2. MARY ELIZABETH, born April 24, 1852, at San José; married Luis F. Emilio (captain U. S. Volunteers, War 1861-5), a native of Salem, Massachusetts, at San Francisco, March 29, 1876.

Issue :

1. LUIS VICTOR, born June 22, 1879; died August 23, 1894.
2. MARGARET BELDEN, born January 28, 1886; died July 26, 1886.
3. GERALD BELDEN, born October 27, 1887; died July 31, 1889.

3. GEORGE FREDERICK, born March 10, 1854, at San José, California; married Anna Humphrey.

Issue :

1. JOSIAH HUMPHREY.
2. LULAH MARGARET.

4. LAURA JANE, born June 5, 1857, at San José; married George Rutledge Gibson, of New York.

Issue :

MARIA LOUISE, born November 24, 1883.

5. LOUISE ARCHER, born July 8, 1859, at San José; married Lewis M. Iddings, of New York.

Issue :

ELIZABETH LAURA, born March 29, 1892.

BEARDSLEY

WILLIAM BEARDSLEY came from England on the ship "Planter," 1635. He was born in 1605; married (in England, probably Stratford-upon-Avon) Mary ——, who was born in 1609.

Children (born in England):

1. MARY, 1635.
2. JOHN, 1637.
3. JOSEPH, 1638.

MARY BEARDSLEY (William^1), born 1635; married, first, Thomas Wells, May, 1651; secondly, Samuel Belding.

MARY WELLS (Mary^2, William^1), eighth child of Thomas Wells and Mary Beardsley; married Stephen Belding, August 1, 1682.

BURT

HENRY BURT, born in England; Roxbury, 1639; Springfield, 1640; married Ulalia ——, who died August 29, 1690. He died April 30, 1662.

Children:

1. JONATHAN, born 1632; married Elizabeth Lobdell.
2. DAVID.
3. NATHANIEL, married, first, Rebecca Sikes; secondly, Mary Ferry.
4. ABIGAIL, married, first, Francis Ball; secondly, Benjamin Munn; thirdly, Lieutenant Thomas Stebbins.
5. MARY, married William Brooks.
6. ELIZABETH.
7. SARAH, married, first, Judah Gregory; secondly, Henry Wakely.
8. PATIENCE, born August 18, 1645; married John Bliss.
9. MERCY, born September 27, 1647; married Judah Wright.
10. HANNAH, married John Bagg.
11. DORCAS, married John Stiles.

223

ELIZABETH BURT[2], married, first, Samuel Wright, Jr., November 24, 1653; secondly, Nathaniel Dickinson, 1684.

CADWELL

THOMAS CADWELL[1], born at Hartford, 1652; married Elizabeth Wilson, daughter of Deacon Edward Stebbins, 1658; died October 9, 1694.

Children:

1. MARY, born January 8, 1659.
2. EDWARD, born November, 1660.
3. THOMAS, JR., born December 5, 1662.
4. WILLIAM, born July 14, 1664.
5. MATTHEW, born October 5, 1668.
6. ABIGAIL, born November 24, 1670.
7. ELIZABETH, born December 1, 1672.
8. SAMUEL, born April 30, 1675.
9. HANNAH, born August 22, 1677.
10. MEHITABEL, born January 12, 1679–80.

MATTHEW[2] (Thomas[1]), son of Thomas Cadwell, born October 5, 1668, at Hartford, Connecticut; married, March 25, 1695, Abigail, daughter of John Beckley (son of Sergeant Richard Beckley, who died August 5, 1690; he was one of the early settlers of Wethersfield); died April 22, 1719.

Children:

1. JOHN, born November 30, 1702.
2. ABEL, born November 27, 1703.
3. DANIEL, born May 18, 1710.

JOHN[3] (Matthew[2], Thomas[1]), born November 30, 1702; married Dorothy, daughter of Thomas Kilborn (and great-

224

grand-daughter of Thomas Kilborn, who was baptized in the parish of Wood Dilton, Cambridge, England, May 8, 1578, and who came to New England in the ship "Increase," which sailed from London April 15, 1635). John Cadwell died April 2, 1746.

Children :

1. JOHN, born 1734.
2. ANN.
3. ABIGAIL.
4. RUTH.
5. DOROTHY.
6. MATTHEW.
7. SUSANNAH.
8. LUCY.

The mother was appointed guardian to the children April 7, 1747.

JOHN[4] (John[3], Matthew[2], Thomas[1]), born 1734; married Abigail, daughter of William Hills (and great-grand-daughter of William Hills and Phillis Lyman, daughter of Richard Lyman); died May 7, 1782.

Children :

1. JOHN, born January 9, 1758.
2. SUSANNAH, baptized October 26, 1760.
3. DAVID, baptized May 26, 1765.
4. ESTHER, baptized December 6, 1767.

JOHN[5] (John[4], John[3], Matthew[2], Thomas[1]), born January 9, 1758; married Annar, who was born October 9, 1762, died February 2, 1835; died March 3, 1834.

"WASHINGTON, DISTRICT OF COLUMBIA, February 25, 1896.

"HON. JAMES J. BELDEN, Syracuse, New York:

"SIR,—In reply to your request for a statement of the military record of John Cadwell, a soldier of the Revolutionary War, I have the honor to advise you that it appears that he performed four tours of service. In May, 1776, he enlisted in Captain Jonathan Well's company, of Colonel Walcot's troops, and served eight months. In March, 1777, he enlisted in Captain Jared Cone's company, Connecticut troops, and served two months. In August, 1778, he enlisted in Captain Richard Pitkin's company of Connecticut troops, and served two months. The service in these three organizations was performed as a private. In July, 1780, he enlisted as a sergeant in Captain Booth's company, of Colonel Hezekiah Wyllys' regiment of Connecticut troops, and served three months.

"During the service he was engaged in Sullivan's retreat from Rhode Island. At the time of his enlistment his residence was East Hartford, Connecticut, and at the date of his application for pension, which was in July, 1832, he resided at Fabius, New York. At that time he was seventy-four years of age. Pension was allowed him.

"Very respectfully,

(Signed) "WM. LOCHREN,

"*Commissioner.*"

Children:

1. JOHN, born April 10, 1783.
2. STEPHEN, born March 11, 1785.
3. ANNAR, born June 15, 1787.

4. CHESTER, born September 18, 1788.
5. BETSY, born March 6, 1791.
6. OLIVE, born February 25, 1794; married, June 6, 1816, Royal Denison Belden; died February 1, 1856.
7. MAHALA, born May 2, 1796.
8. THIRSEY, born June 19, 1799.
9. SHUBIL, who died July 10, 1864.

CHAMBERLAIN

JOSEPH CHAMBERLAIN[1] came to Hadley as a soldier in 1676; removed to Hatfield, 1700; Colchester, 1709, where he died, 1752, aged eighty-seven; married Mercy, daughter of John Dickinson. She died June 30, 1735.

Children:

1. JOSEPH, married, December 26, 1720, Lydia Smith.
2. NATHANIEL, born 1689.
3. SARAH, born November 2, 1690; died young.
4. SARAH, born March 10, 1693.
5. EPHRAIM.
6. RICHARD.
7. JOHN, born in Thetford, Vermont, 1764.

NATHANIEL[2] (Joseph[1]), born 1689; soldier at Fort Dummer; captured by the Indians, September 25, 1727; died November 7, 1780. He married Elizabeth ——.

Children:

1. MARY, born July 13, 1727.
2. SARAH.
3. NATHANIEL, died at Deerfield, August 22, 1745.
4. ELIZABETH.
5. RICHARD.

SARAH[3] (Nathaniel[2], Joseph[1]), married Moses Belding.

Ancestors and Descendants of

DICKINSON

NATHANIEL DICKINSON[1], town clerk and representative; Wethersfield, 1637; removed to Hadley; died there June 16, 1676; married Anna ⁓⁓.

Children:

1. SAMUEL, born July, 1638.
2. OBADIAH, born April 15, 1641.
3. NATHANIEL, born August, 1643.
4. NEHEMIAH, born 1644.
5. HEZEKIAH, born February, 1645.
6. AZARIAH, born October 4, 1648.
7. THOMAS, born March 7, 1667.
8. JOSEPH.
9. JOHN.
10. ANNA.
11. FRANCES, unmarried in 1676.

JOHN[2] (Nathaniel[1]), married Frances, daughter of Nathaniel Foote, of Wethersfield. Their daughter Mercy married Joseph Chamberlain; their daughter Sarah married Moses Belding.

ELY—DAY—BLISS

1. GEORGE ELY, vicar of Tenterden, England, from 1570 to 1615.

2. NATHANIEL ELY, born in Tenterden, 1605. An original proprietor of Hartford, Connecticut, 1635; married Martha ——; died 1675.

3. SAMUEL ELY, born 1659; married Mary Day (daughter of Robert Day, who came from Ipswich, County Suffolk, England, to Boston, April, 1634, in the ship "Elizabeth." An original proprietor of Hartford, Connecticut); died 1692.

4. JOHN ELY, born 1675; married Marcy L. Bliss (daughter of Thomas Bliss, a proprietor of Hartford, "by courtesie of the town," in 1639); died 1758.

5. REUBEN ELY, born 1710; married Lucretia Minor, 1763; died 1799.

6. ESTHER ELY, born 1747; married Captain Silas Childs, of Charlotte County, New York; died ——.

7. LUCRETIA CHILDS, born March 14, 1768; married Samuel Perry, August 4, 1790; died July 22, 1809.

8. SILAS CHILDS PERRY, born February 25, 1793; married Mary Weeks, January 11, 1818; died December 5, 1856.

9. SARAH MELINDA PERRY, born June 18, 1831; married, May 15, 1856, Oscar Edward Van Zile, a descendant of Captain Ferdinand Abram Van Zijl, of the Council of War in New Amsterdam, 1673, and of Thomas Simmons, of Providence, and Sally Bailey, of Nantucket, Rhode Island. He died in Troy, New York, December 18, 1892.

10. JESSIE PERRY VAN ZILE, born November 13, 1857; married James Mead Belden, October 25, 1878.

Jessie Van Zile Belden was educated at the Troy Female Seminary and St. Agnes School, Albany, where she graduated. She is a member of the Emma Willard Association, Vice-Regent of the Onondaga Chapter, D. A. R., and a member of the Society of New England Women.

CASE

JOHN CASE[1] came to this country in 1635. He married Sarah, daughter of William Spencer, of Hartford, Connecticut, about 1657. He lived in Windsor until the spring of 1669, when he removed to Massacoe (now Simsbury). His first wife died November 3, 1691, aged fifty-five, and he married Elizabeth, widow of Nathaniel Loomis, of Windsor, and daughter of John Moore. He was appointed constable by the General Court, October 14, 1669. He was representative to the General Court in 1670 and several times later; died in Simsbury, February 21, 1703–4.

WILLIAM[2] (John[1]), married, 1688, Elizabeth Holcomb, born April 4, 1670.

CAPTAIN JAMES[3] (William[2], John[1]), born March 12, 1693; married, 1715, Esther Fithin; died September 26, 1759.

JEREMIAH[4] (James[3], William[2], John[1]), born July 31, 1726; married Judith Humphrey.

WILLIAM[5] (Jeremiah[4], James[3], William[2], John[1]), born May 23, 1751; married Sarah Hickox; died 1807.

WILLIAM WARREN[6] (William[5], Jeremiah[4], James[3], William[2], John[1]), married Susan Pitney Leonard, who was daughter of John Leonard, born May 21, 1764, and Mary Pitney, born September 5, 1767. She was daughter of Benjamin Pitney and the widow Thompson, née Rysam, and grand-daughter of James Pitney and —— Smythe. Probably the first double wedding in the old church at Morristown, New Jersey, where later Washington worshipped, was that of the brothers Mahlon and Benjamin Pitney, which took place in 1751.

SUSAN MARTHA[7] (William Warren[6], William[5], Jeremiah[4] James[3], William[2], John[1]), born August 8, 1828; married Isaac Pharis, December 14, 1848, who was born May 30, 1823, and who died October 7, 1889. He was the son of Isaac Pharis, born 1796; died July 6, 1845; married Lavina Root, born March 18, 1799; died August 24, 1879.

She was a descendant of Thomas Root (son of John), who was born in England in 1605. He was of Salem, 1637; Hartford, 1639; Northampton, 1654; was one of the seven pillars for the foundation of the church there in 1661. Jacob, the sixth child of Thomas, married Mary, daughter of Samson Frary, of Deerfield, and settled in Hebron, Connecticut.

AUGUSTA[8] (Susan Martha[7], William Warren[6], William[5], Jeremiah[4], James[3], William[2], John[1]), born September 12, 1849; married, September 10, 1872, Alvin Jackson Belden.

GERE

GEORGE GERE[1] was born in England in 1621. He was probably the son of Jonathan Gere, of Hevitree, County Devon. His father died when he was very young, and he with his young brother was shipped to America so that others could inherit the large estate which by law belonged to the orphans. They arrived in Boston in 1636, and were in New London in 1651.

It is a tradition that George Gere was one of the men, under Captain John Mason, who destroyed the Pequot fort at Mystic, June 5, 1637. He was a large land-owner in New London both by grant and purchase. He married, February 17, 1651, Sarah Allyer. He eventually became totally blind, and died at the age of one hundred and five.

ROBERT GERE[2] (George[1]), son of George and Sarah Gere, was born January 2, 1668; married Martha Tyler, who died ——, 1733; died 1742. He was captain and one of the leading men of Groton, Connecticut. All warnings were posted on his mill.

EBENEZER GERE[3] (Robert[2], George[1]), married, January 2, 1735, Prudence Wheeler. She was born September 25, 1712 ; died June 2, 1797.

DAVID GERE[4] (Ebenezer[3], Robert[2], George[1]), born June 2, 1755; married Mary Stanton, May 17, 1781. She died August 31, 1835. He died ——.

ROBERT GERE[5] (David[4], Ebenezer[3], Robert[2], George[1]), born November 20, 1796; married, October 25, 1820, Sophia Stanton ; died December 18, 1877. Their daughter, Mary Anna, married, October 25, 1853, James Jerome Belden.

GOODRICK OF RIBSTON

Arms.—Argent, on a fess Gules between two lions passant gardant Sable, a fleur-de-lis of the field between as many crescents Or.

Crest.—A demi-lion rampant regardant Erminois, holding in his paws a battle-axe Or.

JOHN GOODRYKE[1], of Bolingbroke, County Lincoln, died 1493; married Agnes.

WILLIAM[2] (John[1]), married Jane Williamson ; died 1518.

HENRY[3] (William[2], John[1]), married, first, —— ; secondly, Margaret, daughter of Sir Christopher Rawson.

RICHARD[4] (Henry[3], William[2], John[1]), high sheriff of Yorkshire, 1579; married Clare Norton.

MARGARET[5] (Richard[4], Henry[3], William[2], John[1]), married Sir Francis Baildon, of Kippax, Knight.

RICHARD[6] (Margaret[5], Richard[4], Henry[3], William[2], John[1]), baptized March 25, 1591; died in Wethersfield, Connecticut, 1655.

Royal Denison Belden

HART

STEPHEN HART[1], born in Braintree, Essex County, England, in 1605; came to Boston in 1632, and to Hartford with the Rev. Thomas Hooker.

JOHN[2] (Stephen[1]), born in England; came with his parents; was one of the first settlers of Farmington, Connecticut, and one of the largest planters. He owned not only the farm where his house stood, but also several at a distance. On the night of December 16, 1666, his house was burned, and all the family, with the exception of the son John, perished. Mr. Hart's wife's name was Sarah. All the town records were also burned.

CAPTAIN JOHN[3] (John[2], Stephen[1]), born at Farmington 1655; married Mary, daughter of Deacon Isaac Moore, of Farmington. He was a man of note in Farmington, and died there November 11, 1714. His wife died September 19, 1738, aged seventy-four.

ISAAC[4] (John[3], John[2], Stephen[1]), second son of Captain John), was baptized November 27, 1686; married, November 24, 1721, Elizabeth Whaples. They lived at what was then known as the Great Swamp, afterwards Worthington, and now a part of New Britain. He died January 27, 1770, and his wife, November 14, 1777.

JOB[5] (Isaac[4], John[3], John[2], Stephen[1]), third son and fifth child of Isaac Hart, born January 3, 1731, at Kensington, Connecticut (Worthington); married, March 20, 1755 (by the Rev. Joshua Belden), Eunice Beckley. They removed to Stockbridge, Massachusetts, after the birth of all their children.

233

COMFORT[6] (Job[5], Isaac[4], John[3], John[2], Stephen[1]), eighth son and tenth child of Job Hart, baptized in Kensington, Connecticut, August 25, 1771; married Sibil Churchill, of Stockbridge; admitted to church, 1800. They removed to Pompey, Onondaga County, early in the century, and are buried there.

MIRANDA[7] (Comfort[6], Job[5], Isaac[4], John[3], John[2], Stephen[1]), married Simon Jackson, son of Samuel Jackson, a cousin of Andrew Jackson. She died soon after the birth of her fourth child. Rozelia, the third child, was adopted by Simon Jackson's uncle, Gilbert Jackson.

ROZELIA JACKSON[8], eighth in descent from Stephen Hart, of Braintree, England, was born June 20, 1823, in Pompey. She married, June 23, 1841, Augustus Cadwell Belden, who died March 19, 1896.

KIMBALL

AMOS KIMBALL was born in Haverhill, Massachusetts, 1748; moved to New Hampshire, and died there, September 20, 1820; was a Revolutionary soldier. He married Mary Collis. They had twelve children. The eighth child married Francis Clark. Their daughter, Louisa Clark, married Gardner Woolson, and their daughter, Amelia Gertrude, married Mead Belden, March 31, 1864.

STANTON

THOMAS STANTON[1] came to Virginia from England in the "Bonaventura," 1635. In 1637 he settled in Hartford, Connecticut. He married Dorothy Lord; died December 2, 1676.

Royal Denison Belden

Children:

1. THOMAS, born 1638.
2. JOHN, born 1641.
3. MARY, born 1643.
4. HANNAH, born 1644.
5. JOSEPH, born 1646.
6. DANIEL, born 1648.
7. DOROTHY, born 1651.
8. ROBERT, born 1653.
9. SARAH, born 1655.
10. SAMUEL, born 1657.

CAPTAIN JOHN[2] (Thomas[1]), born 1641; married, 1664, Hannah Thompson. He was in command when Canonchet surrendered. Died in Stonington; will dated 1713.

Children:

1. JOHN, born May 22, 1665.
2. JOSEPH, born June 22, 1668.
3. THOMAS, born April, 1670.
4. ANN, born October 1, 1673.
5. THEOPHILUS, born June 16, 1676.
6. DOROTHY, born 1680.

JOSEPH[3] (John[2], Thomas[1]), born June 22, 1668; married, July 18, 1696, Margaret Chesebro; died 1751.

Children:

1. HANNAH, born December 15, 1698.
2. MARGARET, born October 7, 1701.
3. ZERVIAH, born September 24. 1704.
4. SARAH, born February 22. 1706.
5. ANNA, born August 6, 1708.
6. DOROTHY, born and died July, 1710.
7. JOSEPH, born May 1, 1712.

235

8. JOHN.
9. NATHANIEL.

LIEUTENANT JOSEPH[4] (Joseph[3], John[2], Thomas[1]), born May 1, 1712; married, November 6, 1735, Anna Wheeler; died March 14, 1773.

Children:

1. HANNAH, born August 8, 1736.
2. JOSEPH, born May 31. 1739.
3. MARGARET, born November 3, 1741.
4. ISAAC WHEELER, born January 14, 1743.
5. WILLIAM, born March 5, 1745.
6. ANNA, born February 23, 1747.
7. NATHAN, born December 15, 1749.
8. EUNICE, born November 12, 1751.
9. MARTHA, born November 19, 1753.
10. MARY, born August 28, 1756.
11. DOROTHY, born January 21, 1760.

NATHAN[5] (Joseph[4], Joseph[3], John[2], Thomas[1]), born December 15, 1749. He was an ensign in the Revolutionary War. July 9, 1777, he was with Colonel Stanton, Colonel Barton, six other officers, and thirty-eight privates who went into the midst of the English camp, four miles from Newport, Rhode Island, and captured General Richard Prescott. who was afterwards exchanged by General Washington for General Charles Lee. He married Anna, daughter of General Phineas Stanton; died September 26, 1835.

Children:

1. NATHAN, born July 4, 1779.
2. ANNA, born May 28, 1780.
3. DANIEL, born May 26, 1782.
4. AMOS, born February 11, 1783.

5. ANNA, born December 7, 1784.
6. JOSEPH, born December 20, 1786.
7. BENJAMIN FRANKLIN, born February 12, 1789.
8. ELIZABETH, born April 26, 1791.
9. JOHN JAY, born June 7, 1793.
10. HIRAM, born February 26, 1796.
11. SOPHIA, born November 23, 1798.

SOPHIA[6] (Nathan[5], Joseph[4], Joseph[3], John[2], Thomas[1]), born November 23, 1798; married, October 25, 1820, Robert Gere, son of David Gere and Mary Stanton; died November 16, 1879.

Children:

1. ROBERT NELSON, born June 17, 1822.
2. GEORGE CLINTON, born April 26, 1824.
3. MARY ANNA, born December 14, 1825.
4. A daughter, born October 27, 1827.
5. WILLIAM HENRY HARRISON, born August 14, 1829.
6. NATHAN STANTON, born August 16, 1832.

MARY ANNA[7], born December 14, 1825; married, October 25, 1853, James Jerome Belden.

TAYLOR

JOHN TAYLOR[1] was at Windsor, 1640. He married a widow.

Children:

1. JOHN, born 1641.
2. THOMAS, born 1643.

JOHN[2] (John[1]), born 1641; captain; grantee of Northfield, 1683; settled at Northampton, where he was killed by the Indians. He married Thankful Woodward.

Children:

1. **THANKFUL**, born October 27, 1663.
2. **JOHANNAH**, born September 27, 1665; married, first, Thomas Alvord; secondly, Samuel King; thirdly, Deliverance Bridgman.
3. **JOHN**, born October 10, 1667.
4. **RHODA**, born September 26, 1669; married Samuel Parsons.
5. **ELIZABETH**, born July 13, 1672.
6. **MARY**, born October 13, 1673; married Joseph Atherton.
7. **JONATHAN**, born September 19, 1675.
8. **MINDWELL**, born August 19, 1677; married Jonathan Burt.
9. **LYDIA**, born March 18, 1678; married Samuel Pomroy.
10. **THOMAS**, born November 4, 1680.
11. **ELIZABETH**, born September 17, 1682.
12. **EXPERIENCE**, born October, 1684.
13. **SAMUEL**, born August 30, 1686.

THANKFUL[3] (John[2], John[1]), born October 27, 1663; married, March 22, 1680, Benjamin Wright.

WILKINSON

LAWRENCE WILKINSON[1], born in England; Rhode Island, 1652; married Susannah Smith, daughter of Christopher Smith.

Children:

1. **SAMUEL**, died August 27, 1727.
2. **SUSANNAH**, born March 9, 1652.
3. **JOHN**, born March 2, 1654.
4. **JOANNA**, born March 2, 1657.
5. **JOSIAS**, died August 10, 1692.
6. **SUSANNAH**, born February, 1662.

JOHN[2] (Lawrence[1]), born March 2, 1654; married Deborah Whipple. He died 1751.

Royal Denison Belden

Children:

1. JOHN, born March 16, 1690.
2. MARCY, born June 30, 1694.
3. SARAH, born June 22, 1696.
4. FREELOVE, born July 25, 1701.
5. DANIEL, born June 8, 1703.
6. JEREMIAH, born June 4, 1707.

DANIEL[3] (John[2], Lawrence[1]), born June 8, 1703; married Abigail Inman, a descendant of Edward Inman, September 22, 1740. On the town books of Cumberland he is called Captain Daniel Wilkinson.

Children:

1. JOAB, born July 30, 1741.
2. DANIEL, born July 7, 1743.
3. NEDADIAH, born September 24, 1745.
4. LYDIA, born October 14, 1747.
5. ABIGAIL, born February 9, 1749.
6. A son, born August 6, 1751.
7. JOHN, born November 13, 1758.
8. OLIVE, born March 28, 1761.

JOHN[4] (Daniel[3], John[2], Lawrence[1]), born November 13, 1758; married Betsy Tower, a descendant of John Hancock, who signed the Declaration of Independence.

Children:

1. ELPHA, born October 17, 1783.
2. ALFRED, born July 6, 1786.
3. JOHN, born September 30, 1798.
4. DIANA, born November, 1801.

JOHN[5] (John[4], Daniel[3], John[2], Lawrence[1]), born September 30, 1798; married Henrietta Wilhelmina Swartz. He died September 19, 1862.

Children :

1. JOHN SWARTZ, born August 8, 1827.
2. JOSHUA FORMAN, born June 12, 1829.
3. ALFRED, born August 17, 1831.
4. MARIA HERMANS, born December 15, 1834.
5. THEODOSIA B., born July 16, 1837.
6. JOHN, born February 14, 1840.
7. JANETTE LEE, born September 1, 1841.
8. DUDLEY P., born October 1, 1843.

JOSHUA FORMAN[6] (John[5], John[4], Daniel[3], John[2], Lawrence[1]), born June 12, 1829; married Louisa Raynor.
Children :

1. JOSHUA FORMAN, born March 29, 1861.
2. MARY, born September 19, 1862.
3. THEODORE, born October 5, 1864.
4. REBECCA, born December, 1866.
5. JOHN, born February 11, 1868.
6. FORMAN, born December, 1869.

JOHN[7] (Joshua Forman[6], John[5], John[4], Daniel[3], John[2], Lawrence[1]), born February 11, 1868; married, April 23, 1896, Edith Belden.

WOODWARD

HENRY WOODWARD[1] came from England in the "James," Captain Taylor, 1635; Dorchester, 1639; Northampton, 1659, where he was one of the founders of the church; killed by lightning April 7, 1683; married Elizabeth ——, who died August 16, 1690.
Children :

1. EXPERIENCE, married, November 1, 1661, Medad Pomroy.

2. FREEDOM, baptized 1642.
3. THANKFUL.

THANKFUL[2] (Henry[1]), married, November 18, 1662, John Taylor.

WRIGHT

SAMUEL WRIGHT[2], son of Nathaniel[1], of London, England, deacon; of Springfield, 1639; Northampton, 1655; married, in England, Margaret, who died July 25, 1681. He died October 17, 1665.

Children:

1. BENJAMIN, born 1627.
2. SAMUEL, born 1629.
3. HESTER, born 1631; married Samuel Marshfield.
4. MARGARET, born 1633; married Thomas Bancroft.
5. LYDIA, born 1635; married, first, Lawrence Bliss; secondly, John Morton; thirdly, John Lamb; fourthly, George Colton.
6. MARY, born 1637.
7. JAMES, born 1639.
8. JUDAH, born May 10, 1642.
9. HELPED, born September 15, 1644; died young.

SAMUEL[3] (Samuel[2], Nathaniel[1]), born 1629; killed by the Indians, September 2, 1675; married Elizabeth Burt, November 24, 1653. She married, secondly, September 26, 1684, Nathaniel Dickinson.

Children of Samuel and Elizabeth:

1. SAMUEL, born October 3, 1654.
2. JOSEPH, born June 2, 1657.
3. BENJAMIN, born July 13, 1660.
4. EBENEZER, born March 20, 1663.
5. ELIZABETH, born July 31, 1666.

6. ELIEZER, born October 20, 1668.
7. HANNAH, born February 21, 1671.
8. BENONI, born ten days after his father was killed.

BENJAMIN[4] (Samuel[3], Samuel[2], Nathaniel[1]), born 1660; captain; grantee of Northfield, 1682; a famous Indian-hunter; died 1743; married, first, March 22, 1680, Thankful, daughter of Captain John Taylor, of Northampton (she died April 4, 1701); secondly, Mary Baker.

Children by first wife:

1. BENJAMIN, born February 26, 1681.
2. THANKFUL, born November 13, 1683.
3. REMEMBRANCE, born January 26, 1685.
4. JACOB.
5. MINDWELL, born October, 1694.
6. DANIEL, born April 15, 1697.
7. WILLIAM, born November 26, 1702.
8. MARY, born September 7, 1704.
9. EXPERIENCE, born December 9, 1706.

MINDWELL[5] (Benjamin[4], Samuel[3], Samuel[2], Nathaniel[1]), born October, 1694; married, December 24, 1713, Stephen Belding, Jr.

Index

PART I.—HISTORICAL

Index

Index

PART II.—GENEALOGICAL

Aumack, Chauncey Jerome, 185.
Aumack, James Schuyler, 185.
Aumack, John, 185.
Aumack, John Kingsley, 185.
Aumack, Laura Belden, 185.
Aumack, Lydia Sybil, 185.
Aumack, William Jay, 185.

Bayldon genealogy, 173–222.
Beardsley genealogy, 223.
Beardsley, William, 223.
Belden data, contributed by Mrs. A. A. Ketchum, 187–191, 212–220.
Belden data, contributed by Captain Luis F. Emilio, 220–222.
Belden genealogy, 173–222.
Belden, Alvin Jackson, 180, 231.
Belden, Anna Louise, 180.
Belden, Annaretta, 178.
Belden, Arthur Bevan, 181.
Belden, Ashbel K., 182.
Belden, Augustus, 173, 178, 181, 186.
Belden, Augustus Cadwell, 179, 181, 234.
Belden, Augustus, of Guilford, Vermont, 178.
Belden, Augustus, of Whately, 185.
Belden, Charles A., 186.
Belden, Charles Gilbert, 180, 181.
Belden, Charlotte, 182.
Belden, Chester, 220.
Belden, Corydon, 182.
Belden, Desire, 178.
Belden, Dorcas, 178.
Belden, Edith, 180, 240.
Belden, Edson, 178.
Belden, Edward Mead, 180.
Belden, Edwin, 181.
Belden, Ezekiel Porter, charter member of the Order of the Cincinnati, 215.
Belden, George W., 186.

Belden, Harriet, 179.
Belden, Hiram, 181.
Belden, Jabez, 178.
Belden, James Jerome, 179, 180, 225, 232, 237.
Belden, James Jerome, 2d, 181.
Belden, James Mead, 180, 181, 229.
Belden, Jane Ellen, 182.
Belden, Josiah, of San José, California, 220.
Belden, Julia, 181.
Belden, Laura, 178, 182.
Belden, Lydia, 178.
Belden, Mary, 182.
Belden, Mead, 179, 180, 234.
Belden, Mead Van Zile, 181.
Belden, Merrett, 178, 182.
Belden, Moses, 173, 177, 178, 227, 228.
Belden, Olive, 179, 226.
Belden, Olive D., 182.
Belden, Olive Gertrude, 180.
Belden, Oscar Van Zile, 181.
Belden, Rhoda, 178.
Belden, Richard, 173.
Belden, Royal Denison, 173, 178.
Belden, Rozelia, 181.
Belden, Perry, 181.
Belden, Sally Maria, 178, 184.
Belden, Samuel, 173.
Belden, Schuyler M., 182.
Belden, Sir Francis, 222.
Belden, Stephen, 174, 175, 223.
Belden, Stephen, Jr., 174, 242.
Belden, Wallace Augustus, 182.
Belden, Warren, 182.
Belden, William E., 182.
Benson, Cadwell B., 179.
Benson, Dr. David, 179.
Benson, Elsie A., 179.
Benson, Peter, 179.

246

Index

Index

Taylor, John, 237.
Taylor, Thankful, 238, 241.

Van Zile, Jessie Perry, 181, 229.
Van Zile, Oscar Edward, 181, 229.

Wallace, B. F., 183.
Wallace, Charles, 183.
Wallace, Denison Belden, 183.
Wallace, Ellen May, 184.
Wallace, George W., 183.
Wallace, John Quincy Adams, 183.
Wallace, Joseph W., 183.
Wallace, Seth, 183.
Wallace, Zabina H., 183.
Webster, Ruth, 221.

Wigglesworth, Henry, 180.
Wigglesworth, Silvia, 180.
Wilkinson genealogy, 238–240.
Wilkinson, Helen, 180.
Wilkinson, John, 180, 239, 240.
Wilkinson, Joshua Forman, 240.
Wilkinson, Lawrence, 238.
White, Andrew Strong, 180.
Woodward, Henry, 240.
Woodward, Thankful, 237.
Woolson, Amelia Gertrude, 180, 234.
Woolson, Gardner, 234.
Wright genealogy, 241, 242.
Wright, Benjamin, 238, 242.
Wright, Mindwell, 242.
Wright, Samuel, 241.

THE END

248

www.ingramcontent.com/pod-product-compliance
Lightning Source LLC
Chambersburg PA
CBHW031406270326
41929CB00010BA/1348